MODERN WARRIORS

★ ★ ★

REAL STORIES FROM REAL HEROES

PETE HEGSETH

FOX
NEWS
books

A hardcover edition of this book was published in 2020 by Broadside Books.

All interior photographs, unless otherwise noted, are courtesy of Fox News. For those photographs and images that are the exception, grateful acknowledgment is made to the following: Endpaper flag and pages iv–v: © weyo/stock.adobe.com. Pages ii–iii: © kaninstudio/stock.adobe.com. Page vi–vii: © kaninstudio/stock.adobe.com. Pages xvi–1, 62–63, 112–113,176–177: © bptu/stock.adobe.com. Page 18: photo courtesy of the *Washington Post* via Getty Images. Page 61: © bptu/stock.adobe.com. Page 79: © Prazis Images/stock.adobe.com. Page 95: © Yuriy Seleznyov/stock.adobe.com. Page 114: Lieutenant Commander (Ret.) Daniel Crenshaw. Photo courtesy of Tom Williams/CQ-Roll Call, Inc. via Getty Images. Page 144: photo courtesy of April Pizana Photography. Page 176: photo courtesy of Echo Charles. Page 193: photo © Moshe Zusman 2018. Page 210: photo courtesy of Bill Miles.

HarperCollins books may be purchased for educational, business, or sales promotional use. For information, please email the Special Markets Department at SPsales@harpercollins.com.

FIRST FOX NEWS BOOKS EDITION PUBLISHED 2021.

Imprint and logo are trademarks of Fox News Network LLC.

Library of Congress Cataloging-in-Publication Data has been applied for.

ISBN 978-0-06-304655-9

21 22 23 24 25   FB   10 9 8 7 6 5 4 3 2 1

This book is dedicated to the real 1 percent:
the warriors—past, present, and future—
who answered freedom's call.

CONTENTS
— ★ ★ ★ —

MODERN
WARRIORS

— ★ ★ ★ —

INTRODUCTION
— ★ ★ ★ —

I couldn't take it anymore. I couldn't just sit there and let the help-lessness that had been building overwhelm me.

It was June 2014. I'd been watching the deteriorating reports coming out of Iraq for months. A grim roll call of cities where we'd shed so much American blood was falling under the black flag of the Islamic State (ISIS).

Tikrit.

Mosul.

Fallujah.

Ramadi.

I'd been on Fox News shouting about this dire situation. It was clear that we had an administration at 1600 Pennsylvania Avenue that either didn't care or was intentionally downplaying ISIS as a "jayvee team." The carnage and retreat were not what a generation of warriors fought and bled for. The country of Iraq, and nearby Syria, were rapidly falling to a group of Islamic fighters who were *worse* than al-Qaeda or the Taliban. Had we forgotten the lessons of 9/11 completely?

Worse, that administration didn't seem to give a damn about the impact on America or her warriors. Blinded by political correctness and distracted by domestic priorities, they simply did not believe Islamists wanted to dominate Iraq, Syria, Afghanistan—the region, the world. America's modern warriors, of course, know better.

Somebody had to do something. Too many noble warriors had done too many good things, great things, heroic things, for all of it to be brought down like the Twin Towers—or like the "Golden Dome" in Samarra where I served.

Samarra.

Another town that fell to ISIS. The hometown of their leader, Abu Bakr al-Baghdadi.

On 9/11 I was a college student. Those attacks on New York City, the Pentagon, and in the skies reoriented the trajectory of my life—and the lives of an entire generation.

I was an infantry first lieutenant with my boots on the ground in 2006 when al-Qaeda perpetrated the other strategic attack that altered our war's trajectory. The destruction of the Samarra Golden Dome—a Shia mosque inside a Sunni town—put Iraq in a death spiral of sectarian violence that took many more American lives. Yet, our warriors fought, surged, and overcame. We were willing to make the sacrifice, had committed ourselves to it.

Now the proverbial rug got pulled from beneath our feet. As I sat at my desk in 2014—leading the largest conservative veterans organization in America—I was feeling more profoundly than ever the depressing effects of a premature, and political, withdrawal of US troops. Iraq was the "bad war," according to the Obama administration, so we abandoned the strategic gains of the 2008 surge—undoing all the good that had been done. Iraq was lost, right before our eyes.

Earlier that week, I'd gotten a call from Staff Sergeant David Bellavia, a great friend, a Silver Star guy, Medal of Honor nominee, and general badass. I joked with him that he was a man of ideas—lots of them. Of the fifty he would tell me about, forty-five were crazy, four implausible, and one genius. As he talked, one of those four implausible ones began to transform into the single genius.

David had a plan for how we could turn all of the helplessness, resignation, and outrage that veterans and patriots were feeling into something positive. Like most audacious actions, the idea was drawn partly from history and partly from the one means that most veterans believed in most—taking direct action.

I was committed to David's notion that we form a modern-day Roosevelt's Rough Riders. We'd recruit, raise, and deploy a small force (a Spartanesqe three hundred) to go help fight ISIS alongside allies on the ground. As I used back channels to connect with key people whose views I respected—warriors I had served with—I let them know that it was a crazy idea on the surface, but forming a unit like this would be neither reckless nor rogue. The moment was crying out for a movement of leaders, of men, of warriors. Sure, the actual fight was important, but we would also send a strong signal to all Americans; we could rekindle the doused fighting spirit that all Americans possess. Being on Fox News could serve as a bully pulpit. I had some connections. What did they think?

I also had a track record for unconventional approaches. I'd taken a similarly audacious step back in July 2005. I'd completed my yearlong deployment to Guantánamo Bay and was working as a market analyst on Wall Street. I read a story about a suicide bombing in Baghdad that had killed twenty-seven. Eighteen of the victims were kids under thirteen; one twenty-four-year-old American soldier also paid the ultimate price. As I sat at my comfy desk near the trading floor, I was inundated that day with televised images of the escalating violence. I wasn't fatigued by it; I was motivated. I reached out to one of my few military connections on a long shot, but a good one. He was a company commander in the legendary Rakkasans (187th Infantry Regiment) of the 101st Airborne Division. He had trained me at Infantry School, and now—as he emailed me back almost immediately—he needed a new second platoon leader. I wanted to be his man. We had to navigate through some serious Pentagon red tape, but within three months I'd punched my ticket to Fort Campbell, trained up with my platoon in Kuwait, and was on to Baghdad, Iraq, where we served for four months before being moved up to Samarra.

Our unit was in Samarra when al-Qaeda blew up the Golden Dome, complicating our efforts to dismantle the insurgency, defeat the enemy, and bring our boys home. Like so many others, our unit experienced the whole gamut—conducting foot patrols and kicking down doors, working with city leaders, enduring firefights and receiving death threats. Our warriors did great things on that foreign soil, as well as in Afghanistan where I was an instructor. Like the real 1 percent of my generation—those who wore our nation's uniform—I saw a lot of things, but I also knew that there was a much wider world beyond our platoon. There were other warriors—shadow warriors— who were the 1 percent of the 1 percent, working in the dead of night to strike fear, and death, into our enemies. Special Operators. As the years have gone by, I've learned a lot more about who they are—as we all learned their stories of gallantry and heroism. Every warrior plays their part, from rank-and-file line units like mine, to Special Operators to our eyes in the sky and ships in the sea.

As you probably have figured out, the 2014 Rough Riders brigade never formed. Hearts were willing, spirits were strong, but that wasn't enough to overcome the overwhelming inertia that had so many mired in the bureaucratic bog. We tried hard, but it wasn't to be. Frankly, just trying was therapeutic, if insufficient.

Fast-forward to my time at Fox News. I've been blessed with a platform to share my army background and stories of my service— but I always knew that there were so many others who didn't have that opportunity. I was, and remain, enormously grateful that I could focus on different aspects of the veterans' experience on the air. Still, I wanted to do more to share the untold stories—to dig deeper and provide even more immediate and intimate glimpses into the lives of these everyday Americans who performed extraordinary things. Some sacrificed everything on the battlefield, and others suffered in silence when coming home—to an America that seemed disinterested, distracted, or too distanced from the warriors and the full spectrum of what they faced.

But largely based on reactions to segments on my show—*Fox & Friends*—it became clear to me that my view of the American public—disinterested, distracted, distanced—wasn't fully accurate. Folks did want to know more. They wanted the real story. They wanted to understand. The black flag of ISIS flew for only so long . . . before another crop of American warriors, unleashed by a new president, wiped them off the map. In an odd way, this rise of ISIS, followed by their defeat, crystallized even further the need to tell the long, winding, conflicted, and utterly courageous stories of the men who have been fighting since 9/11. Did we win? Did we lose? Was it worth it? The legacy of warriors is worthy of elevation—a reflection of what we should really value.

It was out of all those moments that the idea for *Modern Warriors* rose. While politicians and the media can whitewash a conflict, the legacy always remains for those who fought there. The warriors who left their families, friends, and comfort to do the dirty work of their country. We need to tell those stories. And then veterans come home, with hopes and dreams—and scars of war. They struggle to transition to civilian life; many are wounded (seen and unseen); many wrestle with post-traumatic stress; suicide was taking more lives than the battlefield ever did. We cannot allow ourselves to look away, to shrug, and say that's just the way it is.

We had to do what we did downrange. We had to embrace the suck. We had to be able to share with our families and our nation the reality of what it meant to be there, to fight, to lose buddies, and to honestly engage in a conversation among ourselves to figure out what all of this meant—and what it means for our country.

The televised *Modern Warriors* specials on Fox News and Fox Nation were the product of an amazing team. One thing motivated us all—our collective desire to get the real story. The ground truth. The politically incorrect version you don't normally get in the 24-hour news cycle. This book is a piece of an ever-expanding puzzle-portrait of our modern warriors: what they witnessed, what they did, and how they *really* feel about all of it. They have a lot to say—and my role in this project is to fade into the background, as I try to do in the shows, and let them have their say. The goal of the televised specials, and this book, is to create the natural environment where veterans feel most comfortable to tell the *real* story—surrounded by peers, with plenty of time, lots of humor, drinks in our hands, and the stories flowing. This book aims to feel like you are having a conversation with them at the bar, just shooting the shit.

By their nature, these veterans are straight talkers. And they have strong, informed opinions. In the company of one another, keeping it in the family, they pull no punches. The same is true here. This book offers you a privileged glimpse into their lives. They share their stories for their benefit, as well as yours. They share a desire to step beyond the boundaries of their immediate military families—to include you.

Each of the chapters in this book highlights an individual modern warrior who has agreed to share experiences and insights. The good, the bad, the weird, the beautiful, the ugly—the real story in their own words, from the interviews I conducted with them. I only interject as necessary for clarity and to make transitions smoother.

My words appear in a typeface that differs from the first-person narratives.

I also grouped their stories around several themes, meant to draw out the similarities and differences among these remarkable individuals. You may choose to read them in order, but you can also dip in and out of sections to get the full spectrum of what our warriors experienced.

I'm privileged to call many of these warriors friends. These are great Americans. They are heroes—even if they reject that title. Working on this venture with them has made me even more proud to be an American—which I didn't know was possible. These men and women are true patriots and true warriors. Like those before them, some may have joined the military for a cause or for the college money, but that soon became secondary to the brotherhood of war. When the bullets start flying, there are no Republicans or Democrats, whites or blacks—only brothers, the greatest of our men and women.

This book is dedicated to everyone who has answered America's call. Who put it all on the line—and especially those who gave the ultimate sacrifice on the altar of freedom.

We never, ever forget them. Warriors forever, in life and death. May their stories live forever.

I've lost so many teammates, but man, they went out like we want to go out, with our boots on. Died putting foot to ass for their country. That's the greatest thing ever.

—*Lieutenant Morgan Luttrell*

★

If you just hit something and tackle it honestly, work it hard, bring new ideas, you can go a long way.

—*Staff Sergeant Johnny "Joey" Jones*

★

I have been very blessed to have a great network of people surrounding me since getting shot and losing my leg. I want to make sure that those veterans coming along after me receive that same gift.

—*Sergeant First Class John Wayne Walding*

★

Being a SEAL team guy was my entire life. It wasn't part of life for me; it was a way of life, and I didn't want to lose that.

—*Lieutenant Morgan Luttrell*

★

I don't want my impact on life to be just that I was a warrior and a soldier. I want it to be that I was a patriot. I served my country. I stood alongside my brothers and sisters in defense of this country. After that, I went out and continued being a model in society demonstrating what you can do even though the cards are stacked against you.

—*Captain Chad Fleming*

PART I

NEVER GIVING UP

I honestly do not have a clue how I made it, how I did it. Got up every day, strapped up every day, and left the wire. Today, I want to come home every day, and my back hurts. I want an Epsom salt bath and to eat some ice cream. I appreciate everything that the guy I was back then did. Who I am today, I don't know if I could do that, to be honest with you.

—*Sergeant Nick Irving*

★

You plan to get injured. You go out there every single night knowing that you're facing an imminent threat.

—*Sergeant Mat Best*

— ★ ★ ★ —

CHAPTER I

SERGEANT FIRST CLASS (RET.)
JOHN WAYNE WALDING
UNITED STATES ARMY

Man, I'm just living the great
American one-legged dream.
If I don't, the guy that shot me
wins; and he ain't gonna win.

Lying on my back, I looked up at the faces of the combat medics as they wheeled me through the med station. I could see the fear in the eyes of these young kids. I'd been medevaced in from Shok Valley, Afghanistan, after a horrendous firefight. I'd taken a round to my right leg that damn near took it right off. It still lay folded like a bird's wing, tucked up into my crotch. My tourniquet had saved my life, but I lost a lot of blood and now I had a new problem. . . . I'd stopped breathing.

Thinking back to right after I was shot, I know I looked down at my leg and saw I had a big problem. My leg was folded over, hanging by an inch of flesh; I had to fix it. I didn't grab my green beret, rub it on my leg, and tell my sergeant that I didn't have time to bleed. I did what any human being would do. I cried. I screamed. After a few seconds, I realized that I had to adapt to this new normal. *I'm going to die if I don't stop the bleeding.*

Now I live by the creed that I'm dumb, but I know I'm dumb, so that almost makes me smart. So I said to myself, *Your leg just got shot off. You better ask for help.* I asked Dave to help me put my tourniquet on. He did the best he could.

After we got that on, I thought, *I'll be danged, Spielberg got it right! It looked just like the movies.* But this was no movie. Blood was spurting out and arcing up in the air. The good thing was, I could see that, so I knew that I had to crank the tourniquet to get it tighter. When I saw the blood stop, I knew that was good.

I also grabbed my morphine injector for the pain. One end of the plastic tube was purple. I couldn't remember what end the needle would come out, so I asked who I thought was the most qualified to answer, my medic.

"Hey, Ron!" I shouted as he attended to the other more seriously wounded guys. "What side is down?"

"Purple!"

I put the purple side down, slammed the injector, and felt a sharp pain in my thumb.

I was pissed and threw my injector at him. "You've got one job, Ron. One job, and you messed it up! I'm going to beat you with my leg when I see you, Ron!"

Midfirefight the whole team was laughing.

★★★★★★★★★★★★★★★★★★★★★★★★★★★★★★★★★★★★★★

There's a saying, "It ain't bragging if it's so," and that applies to John Wayne Walding. He's got a personality as big as Texas and a rare and disarming combination of positivity, vulnerability, and courage. What else to expect from a man with his name and his birthdate—July 4?

Raised forty miles east of Waco in Groesbeck, he laughingly says that his upbringing was something out of *Friday Night Lights*; despite the town's roughly 3,500 population, they had a high school that included a $10 million football field. Like any good Texas country boy, John Wayne did play football, along with baseball and track. His fondest memories were listening to his grandmother sing in the church choir, sitting in a deer stand hunting whitetail, or fishing on a bank next to his grandfather. Those were the times where they instilled the old code of doing the right thing, working hard, and helping others.

He credits his grandparents for helping keep him on the straight and narrow. John Wayne was born to a mother of Mexican heritage and an Anglo father who worked as a roughneck in Texas's oil fields. As John Wayne puts it, "That's Texas right there—tacos and oil rigs."

Unfortunately, both his parents wound up in prison when John Wayne was young. Some of John Wayne's first memories of his father were seeing him in an orange jumpsuit, chained to a gang of ten other guys. His parents were into drugs, marijuana mostly, and were, in his estimation, "good people but bad parents." His grandparents, Sam and Grace Walding, stepped in to fill the void left by John Wayne's absentee parents. The way John Wayne sees it, his parents showed him what wrong looks like, and his grandparents showed him what right looks like. Sam grew up in a dirt-floor shack, dropped out of school, and started working on a drilling rig when he was fourteen. He later went on to run the entire rig. John Wayne believes that's what this country is all about. "My granddaddy showed me to never let life's circumstances dictate your future. That no matter who you are or where you come from, in America, hard work and dedication will always prevail. He's my hero and that is why I named my son after him. Although I did try for John Wayne Junior, but my wife wouldn't have it."

There's another expression: "The apple doesn't fall far from the tree." Sam was just as proud of his grandson as John Wayne is of him, and with good reason. John Wayne served in the US Army for twelve years. For seven of those he was a Green Beret and a member of the 3rd Special Forces Group at Fort Bragg, North Carolina. His tours of duty include Iraq and Afghanistan. He served on ODA 396/3336 as a Special Forces communications sergeant and on the sniper detachment as a sniper instructor.

During 2008's Battle of Shok Valley (Operation Commando Wrath), an enemy sniper's round shattered John Wayne's leg. Eventually it had to be amputated. "Determined" doesn't begin to describe John Wayne Walding. After being wounded, John Wayne attended the Special Forces Sniper Course and became the first amputee ever to become a Green Beret sniper. Using a hand crank, he went on to compete in the 2009 Boston Marathon, in which he finished fourth; he also finished in the top ten in the 2009 New York City Marathon, walked the Bataan Memorial Death March (26.2 miles) with forty-five pounds on his back, and recently ran the Dallas Marathon. During his career, John earned the Silver Star as well as the Bronze Star, the Purple Heart, the Combat Infantryman Badge, the Airborne Air Assault Badge, and the Special Forces Tab. He firmly believes his best accomplishment is marrying his wife, Amy, and raising their four children—Emma, Sam, Andie, and Hannah in Little Elm, Texas.

★★★★★★★★★★★★★★★★★★★★★★★★★★★★★★★★★★★★★★

FINDING A BETTER WAY

At twenty years old, I looked at myself in the mirror. I was still in Groesbeck, working a dead-end job and wanting to get out and see the world and be better. I was tired of being broke. A friend of mine, Clayton Loper, was in the army and he told me about things. I decided to join. What I didn't know was that there was a ten-to-twenty-thousand-dollar enlistment bonus that the recruiters didn't tell me about. So much for that. I was in basic training on 9/11, and a few months later, I was in Iraq as a fire control operator/maintainer. I was excited. I was going to be able to shoot the Patriot missile. It wasn't as cool as it sounds.

Heeding his grandfather's advice, John Wayne wanted to be better once again. He seized an opportunity to go to Fort Bragg. It was there that he heard about the Green Berets for the first time.

Within thirty days he had a selection date, began a rigorous training school for Green Beret candidates, and earned his right to wear the coveted green beret.

On April 6, 2008, John Wayne and the other members of the 3rd Special Forces group were in Nuristan Province on Afghanistan's northeastern border with Pakistan. On that operation, John Wayne was serving as the leader of Assault Team 1. He and Dave Sanders were the lone Americans on that team. They were joined by an Afghani interpreter they called Boo-yah and ten Afghani commandos. Their mission, code-named Commando Wrath, was to kill or capture a high-value target named Haji Ghafour. The military rated the value of targets on a numerical scale, and Ghafour was a 0—the highest, the same as Osama bin Laden. Ghafour and his group were operating in the Shok Valley, and he was thought to be in command of three thousand fighters, all members of a militant group that was threatening to conscript (force to fight in their terrorist organization) all the Afghani men in the Shok Valley.

Ghafour and his men held the high ground above the valley floor, the best position from which to control all traffic in and out of the area. The mountainous terrain was beautiful but deadly. The walls of the valley angled steeply up. Intelligence indicated that the enemy's stronghold was some five hundred feet above the valley that sat ten thousand feet above sea level. The ensuing battle resulted in the awarding of ten Silver Stars for bravery. Not since the Vietnam War had there been that many awards presented for a single action. Later, two of those Silver Stars were upgraded to Congressional Medals of Honor—Special Forces medic Ron Shurer and Special Forces weapons sergeant Matthew Williams earned that distinction. Along with them, Senior Airman Zach Rhyner, the air force combat controller assigned to them, was awarded the Air Force Cross.

INTO THE VALLEY OF DEATH

The village was built into the side of a mountain. The terrain was so rough that the helos couldn't land—too many boulders in the wadi, a narrow ravine where the runoff from the snowmelt was still running. The pilots descended to about ten to fifteen feet above the ground. We jumped out, and I was thinking, *There goes about 10 to 15 percent of our troops*—from twisted knees and sprained ankles. When we did our accountability, we figured out that nobody was hurt.

We began climbing, making our way up narrow goat paths. At that altitude breathing wasn't easy, especially with all the weight we were carrying. Progress was slow but steady. As Assault Team 1, we were in the lead. We got to about forty meters from the building at the outer edge of the village. Next thing I knew, we got opened up on. An avalanche of gunfire tore down on us. I could hear rounds snapping above our heads. We weren't the main target of the assault. They were after the command and control element downhill of our position.

Within the first five minutes, over the comms, I heard that C. K., our lead interpreter, had taken a round in the throat and died on impact. Dillon Behr, a Special Forces radio operator, was shot in the hip, and the medic estimated he had about twenty minutes until he bled out. I knew that given the situation he wasn't likely to make it. We weren't going to be able to get down that mountain. We weren't going to be able to suppress the enemy's fire to get a medevac bird in time to get there.

A few minutes later, word came in that Luis Morales had been shot twice in the leg. At that point, we knew we weren't going to be able to climb any higher. We had to get down; we had to get to where the command and control element was, where the fire was being directed. We were going to have to initiate Operation Human

Shield—using our bodies to catch the bullets while Ron Shurer, our only medic, was working to keep the two wounded guys alive.

A LIFE CHANGED IN AN INSTANT

That worked out pretty well, until about two and a half or three hours into this thing. I was moving from one position to another when suddenly my right leg went out from under me. I fell forward, rolled over, and looked down at my leg. It was just hanging there at a 45-degree angle, held there by an inch of flesh. I was in serious pain, lying there screaming, crying, and looking to my brothers for help.

Dave Sanders came over to me and helped me get my tourniquet on. It took a bit of adjusting to get it to do its thing, but eventually my leg stopped spurting blood. I grabbed my weapon, low-crawled into a firing position, and rejoined the battle.

A while later, Ron was still attending to Dillon and Luis. I could see him hunched over those guys and I was thinking that so far, I was the only one really taking care of me. I wasn't qualified to keep me alive. So I said, "Hey Ron, come check me out, bro!"

I'll never forget him peeking his peanut head over Dillon and giving me a thumbs-up and saying, "You're good."

"Screw you, Ron! I'm not good. I know me when I'm good; this is not good!"

Later it dawned on me that Ron figured that if I could yell at him like that, I was good. And Ron was great that day, CMOH [Congressional Medal of Honor] great, even if he didn't know what color was the pointy end.

I grabbed my weapon and resumed firing. The thing was, though, even with the morphine in me, every time I moved, my leg caught on something and I felt the most excruciating pain. That had to stop. So

I figured the best thing I could do to keep that leg from snagging on things was to fold it up into my crotch. I held it there between my thighs and resumed firing.

At one point, about ten feet away from me, my team sergeant, Scott Ford, got shot right in the breastplate. He went down to one knee but kept on fighting. I always say that Chuck Norris wears Scott Ford underwear because that's how cool my team sergeant is. Unfortunately, a few minutes later, a shot missed his body armor, and I will never forget seeing his left triceps just kind of filet off the back.

HELP FROM ABOVE

There were about ten of us left on that mountainside. That's when every air asset in the vicinity came in, dropping two-thousand-pound JDAMs and doing gun runs at what we call "danger close," but this was danger closer—about a hundred yards from our position.

I was glad to have them coming in, but with their targets being above us, the mountainside became our enemy, too. A mountain is a big rock. When you drop bombs on it, you make smaller rocks. And when you're underneath them, gravity hates you. Now we're contending with rocks and bullets.

This was all just crazy, but we had to get down to the valley floor. The only way to do that was to follow the goat paths for a bit. The trails were like a series of staircases. We couldn't stay too exposed, so we'd slide/fall down off of one minicliff onto another perch and then slide/fall again, until we got to the bottom. Wash, rinse, repeat. I couldn't walk, and crawling maybe three inches at a time wasn't going to do, so other guys had to drag me along while I was carrying my own leg.

Ron was helping me down the mountain at one point, and I

could see that I was bleeding all over him. He said, "Really, bro? This was my favorite shirt!"

That was the kind of banter that got us all through that bit of hell.

At the valley floor, my teammates were carrying me on a litter. That wadi was a flowing river of snowmelt, but we had to get across it. It wasn't deep, but man it was cold! I was thinking, *Come on, baby Jesus. I've survived a gunshot. Now you're going to make me die of hypothermia?*

When the medevac bird came in, Scott was about to board. I was lying there watching this, watching that bird lower into the valley floor. A few seconds later, we heard the pilot screaming, "I'm hit! I'm hit!"

Under relentless gunfire, I had to get dragged away from that open ground, across the freezing water again, and wait for another helicopter to come in. Even the second bird wasn't enough to get us home. We had to execute an emergency landing because the helo received too much damage getting us out of Shok. We cross-loaded into a third medevac bird that successfully got us to the combat hospital in J-Bad.

When I suddenly stopped breathing, that was terrifying. When you can't breathe, you can't yell "I need help!" I grabbed the shirt of the soldier working on me, pulled him close, and pointed at my mouth. He got the message. The last thing I remember is a team of them holding me down while cutting through my rib cage for multiple chest tubes.

A GRATEFUL MAN: A CHANGED MAN

God saved my life that day. Dave Sanders helped with that, and we talked this April 6, the anniversary of my injuries. I cherish that relationship with him and thank God that we both made it out alive. I gave Ron a lot of grief back then, but the man had his hands full and he helped save the lives of many guys that day. I can joke about that stuff with my team, but socially I can't joke about the tolls of war. Taking someone's life is not a fun thing to do. It's never a joking deal. Combat brings out the worst in everybody. It's not glamorous. It's the most unforgiving thing in the world.

The day after Shok, I never will forget waking up, looking at ceiling tiles—I know I was procrastinating. I didn't want to look down, because I knew what had happened. I knew that I carried my damaged leg down the mountain, but I also kind of did the whole Ricky Bobby "But with advances in modern science and my income, maybe they could have saved the leg." I've always been a fun-loving, cocky, joking kind of guy, but when I looked down and saw only one foot sticking up at the end of that hospital bed, I started to cry. I was in tears because everything I'd worked for was, in my mind, over.

Our culture needs to accept vulnerability a little bit better. I always say, "They teach you how to deal death, but not deal with it." I can look you in the whites of the eyes, pull the trigger, and sleep well at night, but I can't get that call that Ryan Savard's dead or Aaron Blasjo's dead or Chris Kyle's dead, or all the guys that I know that I've been in service with. We don't know how to deal with that.

What if I'm alive, but I'm not this sweet Green Beret that can climb mountains, jump out of airplanes, do all the SF-guy things? Now I am a one-legged man that can't walk. And that word "can't" is one of the most debilitating words that these guys, including myself, will ever have to deal with, whether you can't go downrange anymore, you can't avenge this guy's death, or you can't do this or that. It's a heck of a psychological disability, really.

I. CAN'T. WALK.

Accepting that undeniable truth was the most devastating, humbling, and terrifying feeling I have ever had to overcome.

That is the true obstacle standing in your way of greatness. It's not a physical limitation like my amputation, it's the mental/psychological challenge of overcoming fear inside like, for me, those three words. *I. Can't. Walk.* There are motivational speakers that say there's no such thing as "can't." In the famous words of *The Office*'s Dwight Schrute, "*False.*" I can never walk again like I used to. For the rest of my life, no matter how much effort I give, the same effort that in my case was enough for me to become a Green Beret, it will never be enough to make me walk. Not without the aid of a prosthetic. But it doesn't mean you're done. There's still so much good you can do. You've just got to figure out what path God has put you on and trust it is the way.

"Can't" is a tough pill to swallow, but that fear/doubt lives right next door to this: "Lean forward, fight hard." I had a sergeant major at Fort Bragg, the absolute epitome of a bad dude that ate nails and shit ice cream. He was a great leader. I will never forget when he said, "All right, men, when you're in combat and your back is against the wall, you've got to lean forward and fight hard." So that thought lives in one house right next to "can't." Sometimes the two of them get along. Sometimes they butt heads. It's your choice who wins.

For example, after my amputation I chose, over fear/doubt, to lean forward and fight hard. While at the sniper detachment, I decided I was going to qualify as a sniper. No one cut me any slack, and I did everything as the rest of the candidates did but one-legged. In fact, most of my classmates (and instructors) didn't even know I had one leg until we were in the field changing into ghillie suits for stalking lanes. When they saw the carbon fiber and titanium, they said, "I could not even tell!" And during our run-and-gun evaluations, I'll never forget telling our class "Don't let the one-legged guy beat ya." I never finished last.

I did have a come-to-Jesus moment there. I realized it was very vain for me to go back onto a team because no matter how good I was on one leg, a Green Beret with two legs will always be better. It wasn't about me. It was about the team. If I ever put one of my teammates in a predicament and they got injured or, heaven forbid, their life was taken because of my injury, I couldn't live with myself. That was when I realized that God had different plans for me, and boy were they great.

STILL LEARNING

The most positive change I ever made in my life is when I decided to stop being good and to start being great. It was a long, difficult road getting there and a decision I must make daily. I took a first step toward being great when I was still recovering from my injury at Walter Reed. I was alone with my son Sam who was at the time only two years old. Being a good dad, I was letting him stand on the coffee table. Maybe I was teaching the one-day airborne paratrooper how to PLF (parachute landing fall). I will never forget watching my son fall off the table onto the floor while I was trying to catch him mid-fall. I remember landing on my stump and feeling excruciating pain.

However, the feeling that was even worse was knowing why. I let my son fall because I was too medicated to react in time. Remember that when a service member is injured, they are too overwhelmed with meds to fix everything. Well, I was on about ten different meds, and it made me a zombie. I knew then I had two choices: pain or pills. I chose pain and vowed to get off all my meds. To this day I am in pain, but I am fine with that. It reminds me of the blessing of being alive and present in my family's life.

My next, and maybe the hardest, step toward being great was after a dear friend of mine was killed in 2013. I was at Bragg signing out of the army and got the horrible call that Chris Kyle (aka American Sniper) had been murdered. At the time I was the lead instructor for Chris's company Craft and we had become close. On a side note, I thought it was awesome the Navy SEAL needed a Green Beret to teach for him.

After hanging up the phone I did what every soldier feels is the right thing to honor a fallen comrade's life: I drank. The next morning, I remember waking up with feelings of sadness, anger, and determination. You know what? Enough. Enough. If his life, if all the lives of the guys I've lost matter so much to me that I've got to do this, then by goodness I owe it to them to live well. At the time I made this decision, it really wasn't about drinking. It was about living well. I realize that Chris didn't have a choice anymore. But I did. And for Chris, all the rest of the guys who lost their lives, all the guys I knew and didn't know who were struggling, I owed it to all of them to be great. It was then I took the next step. Sobriety.

I also owe it to the American people. Having people say thank you to me for my service helped me heal. My leg will never grow back, so the support I get from great Americans motivates me to keep wanting to be great. People ask me all the time if what I did over there was worth it. The thank-yous make it worth it. That's why

I never say "You're welcome" in return. I always say, "You're worth it." You are worth the sacrifices, you are worth the holidays, you are worth the birthdays that I've had to spend downrange. And for the brothers I miss and this leg that will never grow back—you're worth it. And thank you.

★ ★ ★

CHAPTER 2

STAFF SERGEANT (RET.)
JEREMIAH WORKMAN
UNITED STATES MARINE CORPS

I've been blessed. I made
it through Fallujah. I made
it through PTSD. I came out
on the other side. I'm still
here. I'm still kicking.

Even though it was the middle of the afternoon, the dust and smoke were so thick that it seemed like the sun was on the verge of setting. Through that dense air, I could barely see past my extended arm. We'd been exchanging gunfire for I don't know how long. Each side must have tossed a dozen grenades by that point. The hooked stairway we'd tried to climb was like a slick mountainside. We'd get up only so far before their bullets pushed us back down the slope.

Just ahead of me was Phil Levine. I saw him bring the muzzle of his rifle up slowly; then it dropped. He did that a couple of times. I knew he'd been hit but he wouldn't listen to anybody who tried to tell him to get the hell out of that building to get treated. I put my hand on his back and he turned to me. In the dim light, his face was pale, his lips blue. I'm no doctor but I knew that he had to be losing a lot of blood. Your lips turn blue when you're cold, and it was hotter than hell inside that house. I tried to talk him into getting out. My words got drowned out by more gunfire. Phil still couldn't raise his rifle high enough to sight on a target. The next thing I knew, he had reached out and taken the unused pistol from the man laying down rifle fire in front of him. That man did what a warrior does. He'd raised his right hand and said that he would support and defend the Constitution of the United States. Like the rest of us, he was there in Fallujah for that reason. More than that, he loved his country; he loved his platoon mates. He was a patriot. When I think of that concept, I put his name, his face, right beside that word.

★★

Marine corporal Jeremiah Workman also deserves the title "warrior and patriot." For his actions during a firefight on December 23, 2004, he earned the Navy Cross (the marines' and navy's second-highest medal of distinction for heroism in combat) while serving as a squad leader with the marines' 3rd Battalion, 5th Marine

Regiment. He and the other members of his unit were especially motivated that day. Many of their fellow marines were isolated within a building that was being cleared. Workman and others worked tirelessly to first allow three of those marines to escape. Risking his own life repeatedly, Workman exposed himself to enemy gunfire. An enemy grenade exploded directly in front of him. He sustained shrapnel wounds to his arms and legs. Though wounded, he led a third assault on the enemy's position and helped extract more marines. Eventually, he contributed to twenty-four insurgents being eliminated.

Another number took on even greater importance in Workman's life. He is among the eight out of every one hundred veterans who suffer from post-traumatic stress disorder. He was willing to come forward and share his experiences at a time when the stigma associated with PTSD was at its highest. He continues to educate and to serve other veterans in his role as a military services coordinator for the Veterans Administration at a Naval Health Clinic.

He's not alone in that commitment. His wife, Jessica—they were high school sweethearts in Marion, Ohio—is also fully engaged in spreading the word about PTSD and relationship issues that arise in veterans' lives. Together they've attended a number of retreats sponsored by organizations like Operation Heal Our Patriots-Samaritan's Purse. A dedicated family man, Jeremiah credits the birth of his son as a turning point in his transition from military to civilian life and in dealing with his PTSD diagnosis: "He gave me hope. He gave me a reason to live, to want to live, to be a good dad, to be a mentor. I want both my kids to look up to me." Though he believes that no one is ever "cured" of PTSD, he says that it can be controlled—and it's up to him to be the one to do that. By raising his hand to defend the Constitution of the United States and to let others know that he was struggling with the symptoms of PTSD, Jeremiah Workman has dedicated his life to the service of others.

★★★★★★★★★★★★★★★★★★★★★★★★★★★★★★★★★★★★★★★

Seeing so many of my teammates step up during that ambush, and then on our assault to counteract it, made it easier for me to step up. We train a whole lot and that was great preparation, but what really kicked in for me that day was a survival instinct—to make sure I lived, but more important, to make sure my teammates and my platoon mates lived. Something took hold of me. I had to do what was necessary to take care of the men to the left of me and to the right of me. So even when that grenade went off and I was bleeding from my limbs, I hardly thought about that. I couldn't really take too much time to think; all I had was time to do. I just had to hope that the choices I was making were the right ones. The only thing I knew for certain was that my motivation was right. Instinct took over, and I moved toward the sound of the gunfire. I wasn't the only one, not by any means, and the best thing was seeing our team work well together. It was an amazing pleasure to see us all shoot, move, and communicate the way that we did when the shit hit the fan.

What made that all better is that we had people from all over the country, all walks of life, religions, colors. None of those things mattered. We had one objective: to get our fellow marines to safety. Everything was coming at us at a hundred miles an hour, and we were all adapting and thinking quick on our feet. We were making sound, quality decisions to keep people alive. I felt like I had done the best I could. Nobody's perfect in those situations, and if you could rewind the clock, you might do a few things different.

THE RESPONSIBILITIES OF LEADERSHIP

Arriving at that "nobody's perfect" perspective required many other hard-fought battles to be waged. What made them even more difficult was that not everyone came out alive that afternoon in Fallujah.

That was the toughest thing for me to go through in my life to this point; we lost three marines from my platoon that day. Nothing can prepare you for that. You go to war knowing that it could happen, but until it happens—you just . . .

I remember when we left Camp Pendleton for that deployment. A lot of families and loved ones were there to send us off. Some knew I was a leader, some didn't. Not that it mattered. A few people said to me, "Take care of my son." I'd nod and say, "Yes, sir." Or "Yes, ma'am. We're all going to be okay."

Then you get over there and something really bad happens like it did—losing those three marines and getting a few other guys wounded—and it just breaks your heart. No, it rips your heart right out of your chest. But what's really weird about it is that when you're still there, you really don't have the time to think about it, to process it. We lost those guys in December, and we were still in country until the following April. We lost those marines, but the mission didn't stop. We didn't have the time to sit down and think and mourn those guys.

When you get back to the states, it hits you. A lot of my PTSD issues have to do with survivor's guilt. Nothing can prepare you for watching buddies die in combat. It's just a terrible thing.

To come home and to have that reality hit you upside the head and have you thinking, *Hey, we lost three marines there. You're home, but these other guys, they're not home. They're not with their families, they're not . . .*

I felt a lot of weight on my shoulders.

As the years have gone by and I've worked with a lot of therapists, I can now look back believing that no decision I made that day, or that anyone else made that day, could have saved the lives of those marines. I still do a lot of what-ifs—if we could have gotten to them sooner, gotten into that hidey-hole of a bedroom sooner, maybe. . . .

I run a lot of scenarios through my mind every day.

And I have had to be told, and I have had to learn, that the reality is that people die in combat. All you can do is control what you can, and do the things that you believe and that you have been told will do the most to ensure that everyone comes out alive. Not everyone did come out alive. It's tough not to beat yourself up over it. But if you don't wrap your arms around the fact that you did everything you could, then the failure to recognize and accept that will wind up killing you.

SHARING HIS PERSPECTIVE

As bad as I've had it with PTSD, I'm still grateful. I go around and talk to various groups, and I've never encountered any kind of negativity toward me or what I was asked to do over there. Everyone has been very grateful and very gracious. If there was anything good that can be said about 9/11 it is that it felt like our nation came together in its aftermath. I can't say that's true now. We're all over the damn place. People can't stand each other. I don't get that.

After 9/11, it was like I imagine things were during World War II, when everybody dropped what they were doing to assist in the war effort.

What else breaks my heart is what we did as a country to our Vietnam veterans. I have several friends who served in Vietnam. What they experienced when they returned is just criminal. I wouldn't wish that on anybody.

My maternal grandfather, Ralph McInnis, was awarded a Bronze Star and a Purple Heart. Like many of the Greatest Generation, he never talked much about his exploits, so I don't know what he did to earn such high honors.

A FAMILY TRADITION

I was a big fan of Vietnam movies when I was a kid. I loved *Hamburger Hill*. I'd watch that movie, put on a pair of Dad's old cammie pants, and play war in the yard. I was always wearing my dad's gear and asking him questions. My son is getting to be that age when he's started to ask me about my service. I don't go into the tough details, but we do talk about life in the military and what I did.

A while ago, I was able to take my family to a joint navy–marine corps base outside of Dallas. They put my son in an F-18 simulator and then a C-130 simulator. The smile on his face was just . . . it just made me . . . what can I say except that he hasn't stopped talking about it since? I would never push my son into doing something he wasn't into doing, but I have to say, I would love for him to carry on the family tradition.

It's funny, but as much as I was into the military and war as a kid, I didn't realize until pretty late that there were different branches of service like the army and the marines. It was in junior high that I had my moment of recognition. At the time, recruiters from the various branches would come to the schools, so I understood that part of the equation. One day, I was in the cafeteria eating and this marine walked in wearing his dress blue uniform. Every head in the place turned and followed him, including mine. *Man, that's pretty badass!* I told myself. I could picture myself wearing that thing.

He did have a hard time picturing himself as a hero deserving of the Navy Cross. But he is, and he received it in May 2006 at Parris Island, South Carolina. He had worked there as a drill instructor as part of his nine years of active duty service. It was presented by the commanding general of Parris Island, Brigadier General Richard T. Tryon, at the same time as Sergeant Workman's recruits were graduating from basic training.

IT'S NOT ABOUT ME

The whole thing was kind of a double-edged sword for me. A long time had passed since the events themselves. I'd never read the citation, and there I was standing in front of everyone, hearing it for the first time. So many things were running through my mind, replaying some of what happened. A tear ran down my cheek as I was listening to the master of ceremonies read through all the details. I kept wondering, *Why am I getting this?* Not that I didn't feel like I deserved it—I had been the point man on the stack that went up those stairs all those times—but this wasn't about me. Those marines who lost their lives, they should have been the ones getting it. Obviously, my thoughts were all jumbled up at the time. They were for a while after, and kind of still are. I didn't wear the medal for two months after getting it. Only then I did it because I was told I had to. Today, it's in a closet. People have asked to see it, or they've told me that I should have it in a shadow box on display in my house. I can't do that. It's just not about me. It's more important to keep the memory alive of those three marines—Raleigh Smith, James Phillips, and Eric Hillenburg. I have their names tattooed on my back, but I can hardly put that on display all the time!

Whenever I'm asked, or whenever I do any kind of presentation, I like to talk about them. There's lots of ways to keep their memory alive. One of them for me is to just be the best person I can. Working within the VA, I go to work knowing that I'm helping people that wore the same shoes as I did. They've had to deal with PTSD, with traumatic brain injuries, with many other issues related to serving and then transitioning out of the military. I don't want anything in return but the satisfaction of helping them land on their feet, navigate a complex system. I had so many people help me. I just want to pay it forward.

My early struggles with PTSD were made more difficult by the fact that I had never heard of it before. I credit the marines, traditionally one of the most badass/hard-nosed branches of the army, with having an enlightened view of the diagnosis. They knew the importance of not letting those soldiers who were either diagnosed or self-identified as sufferers be stigmatized.

DANGER CLOSE ALL THE TIME

Jeremiah and his platoon lost three men to enemy fire in December 2004. They were among the seventy-two service members killed in action that month. Fourteen of those (roughly 20 percent) were killed by IEDs. The following month, the period during which that unit didn't have time to come to grips with the death of their teammates, the number of American deaths in Iraq rose to 127, and the number of IED-related deaths more than doubled to 29. Until they left in April 2005, the percentage of deaths by IED stayed well above that 20 percent and stayed there long after.

When I think back on my time in Fallujah, the thing that stands out is that the enemy didn't wear uniforms. Anyone and anything were a potential threat. Once you got back inside the wire, you didn't have time to relax, drink a beer, and get away from the war for a moment. Our positions were coming under mortar attack; out on patrol, we had to worry about IEDs on the way to the objective and on the way back. We were constantly on edge and that takes a toll. I like to have a fighting chance, and that enemy didn't stand a chance against us if they came at us in a traditional way. They knew that. They had to get an edge on us, so they used IEDs. Most of us thought it was cowardly bullshit, but that's what they had to do. They just couldn't go toe to toe with us.

I'm not blaming anybody, but at that time we weren't in up-armored vehicles, unless you count the sandbags on the floor and what we called "ghetto armor" hanging off the sides. Later, in 2007, when I went back as a sergeant, we had the mine-resistant ambush-protected vehicles and that helped a lot. We adapted. That's what we do.

Still, me going from combat to drill instructor was not a smart move. I was trying to be motivated and eager and do something different and get my mind off of Fallujah. I just did that too soon after being over there. Part of what you do as a drill instructor at Parris Island is to break down the individual so that you can build them back up to make them marines. I really struggled with the breaking-down part. I knew that all of those recruits, because of where we were in the war, were likely to end up in a combat situation. I felt like I would better serve them, and me, if I could just talk to them and help them understand what they needed to do to be the best at what was needed in combat. It all felt so personal to me. I wanted to be a big brother to them, and yelling and screaming at them didn't seem like the approach for me at that point in time, given what I was dealing with.

A CHANCE AND A CHANGE

My performance as a drill instructor suffered because I was so in conflict, but the good news was that I got diagnosed with PTSD. And it wasn't just that I was struggling with my job: I was having the worst nightmares, dealing with insomnia and depression.

The other great thing for me was that following my diagnosis and early treatment, I got sent to Quantico. There I met one of the most important figures in my life, Sergeant Major Carlton Kent, who was the sixteenth sergeant major of the marine corps. I was working at the National Museum of the Marine Corps as a kind of guide/show pony. I was a mess, having no real direction for my career and dealing with those pretty heavy personal issues. Even though the marines were doing their best to not make me feel like I was broken, I did feel like a broken toy.

I'll never forget this. I was with Sergeant Major Kent at a Subway in Quantico. He said, "Hey. I want you to come work for me. You're not broken. You're dealing with things that humans deal with when they've been through the shit you've been through." I had heard similar things from various counselors and therapists, but it was different coming from him.

I went to work as his driver, and just having him take a chance on me, to trust me, was huge. To this day, he's like a father to me. We talk every day. He calls me his son. I call him Dad or Pop. He eventually got to know my wife and my kids. He loves my wife. We're all family.

He helped me get in some good treatment facilities and programs.

He and the commandant of the marine corps at the time, General James T. Conway, helped set a positive tone for guys like me. I still repeat this to others all the time: "Hey, it's okay to raise your hand and get help. You don't have to be ashamed. You don't have to lie in the barracks depressed and afraid to tell anybody what you're going through. We're here to help you, and we're going to make sure you get what you need to get better."

I also want to let other veterans know that life is too short to live in pain and suffering. And you don't want to—and you don't have to—make others suffer along with you. PTSD affects your family, your wife, your kids. Deep down, you don't want to do that to them; that's not who you are at your core. By helping yourself, you're helping them. General Conway and Sergeant Major Kent also did a lot to let us all know that we didn't need to worry about our careers, and how a PTSD diagnosis was going to affect our service record and all that. No shame and no blame.

It hurts me a lot to know that twenty-two service members a day die by suicide. This PTSD stuff is real. I know that some people don't think that, but I know what I've seen and what I've experienced. I know that a lot of vets don't want to get treatment. I know that lots of families do everything they can in their power to help that vet get the help needed. It's tough.

THE SILVER LINING

In a weird way, that attitude of not wanting to get help and tough it out is what also makes our veterans and current service members so great. Resilience. A lot of times you get dealt a bad hand, but you tough it out and come out the other side of it better for having done so. I think that anybody who knows me would tell you that I'm compassionate. I'm caring. I love my family. I love my friends. I want to keep doing what I did in the marines. If I could have, I would have stayed in for the full thirty years. I loved being a marine. I miss being with marines in the way that I was on active duty.

Some things are different now. One thing isn't: I still want to serve. I want to continue to make a difference. I don't want to be known only as that guy who did those things in Fallujah. I want to continue to put other people and their needs ahead of me and my own needs.

I just keep moving forward and trying to be happy.

I had so many people who helped me and supported me. I want veterans to know that no matter what time it is, what day it is, how dark they might be feeling, they do have people in their lives who are willing to listen and to help. I'm one of them. There are thousands of others.

I found out through all I went through that I was stronger than I ever thought. So are they.

I tell my son that I was fortunate to serve with a great group of heroes. They're still heroes. We still need them. We're still proud of them, no matter what.

CHAPTER 3

STAFF SERGEANT (RET.)
JOHNNY "JOEY" JONES
UNITED STATES MARINE CORPS

I loved the pain and misery and hard work of doing brick and block masonry alongside my daddy. It was 100 degrees, sweat in your eyes, cuts all over you, hands bleeding, but you're getting the job done. End of the day, wipe the sweat out of your eyes and look back and see that you've built something with your hands that's going to be there long after you're dead.

So about two and a half months into this deployment in Afghanistan, on the same night, we had two different incidents. One of our guys got killed, and another guy got his legs blown off, and both of their teammates got fragged, so we lost four EOD (Explosive Ordnance Disposal) techs out of country in one night. And that's when it really got real. I had put other dudes on the bird. I had been there. My first day working, I picked up the pieces of a guy that was a triple amputee. I had seen the cost of war and the damage these bombs do. But it wasn't until one of my guys died from it, doing the job I do, that it really hit home. At the time, I was big into physical training (PT). And when you're in country and you don't have a gym and you're big into PT, you run a lot. And I remember coming in from running circles around the helo pad, taking my socks off, and my feet were bleeding. And I realized, somewhere in the back of my mind, that the threat of not dying but losing my legs was so big that I had almost accepted it, and I wanted to run every step I could in case I didn't get to run again.

A few months later I went on an offensive operation called Roadhouse II. I knew that that one was going to be a bitch. And I was one of six EOD techs, and we were taking this town only because it was full of IEDs. The cards were stacked against me. I called everybody I cared about and told them, "You're not going to hear from me for a couple of weeks, and if you don't hear from me, that's a good thing." And two weeks later, I didn't have legs.

★★

Johnny "Joey" Jones was born to hardworking and hard-living Georgians who can trace their roots back six generations. The family wasn't dirt poor, but they were old-school Appalachian.

They might have acted like outlaws, but they also served their country when drafted during the Vietnam War. Joey doesn't recall anyone discussing that service, but his grandmother spoke fondly of Joey's great-grandfather, who was a marine. As the oldest of three sons, Joey's father, Joseph Edgar Jones, favored the Irish Cherokee side of the family. He was five feet eight and powerfully built and, despite his penchant for drinking, was a wonderful provider who took that role seriously.

"Work came first, family second, and if there was time for anything else, that was okay. He felt like he had to suffer and do without so that other people could be safe, happy, and cared for."

Joey's dad believed that the raising of young children was up to his wife, Joyce, so Joey had a somewhat strained relationship with his father. When he was old enough to work with his dad, Joey saw him in a new light. That continued as Joey grew older, and he appreciated the lessons of hard work and its rewards.

Joey also credits his father with his interest in football. A die-hard Georgia Bulldogs football fan, Joey played throughout his youth and into high school, where he excelled as an undersize lineman. Joey's grandfather, Johnny Edgar Jones, and his uncle, Jeff Jones, also introduced him to dirt track automobile racing—super-late-model style. "My youngest uncle gave me the fun side of my personality; my grandfather was the wise and smart version; my dad was the hardworking and disciplined example."

Racing was a fixture of family life, as were shared meals, barbecues, and the rare vacation. That closeness was made possible by each of Joey's two uncles and his father living on separate parcels of a five-acre-lot his grandfather had purchased and divvied up among his three sons.

Joey was identified early on as a gifted student, but he lacked both the interest and work ethic to take full advantage of those skills. He graduated from high school mainly because he had to stay academically eligible to compete in sports. By the time he was sixteen, he was also working and primarily financially and socially independent. Other than a yearly opportunity to dine at a steak house with his grandfather, Joey didn't eat in restaurants. At one point, when he was sixteen, the family of the girl he was dating invited him to join them at a LongHorn. "I called her and asked her, 'What do I wear?' I had no clue. That was the kind of life I lived." That girlfriend, her family, and other football families welcomed Joey into their homes and he got a glimpse of a different life—not better, in his mind, just different.

A brief stint at college gave way to a desire to earn full-time wages. Joey had no aspirations beyond life in Dalton, Georgia. Then his girlfriend broke up with him, he was no longer in college, and he took a chance on himself. Two childhood friends had military connections, and he decided to join the marines. "My family had put a lot of work into me. I was the first person in my family to graduate from high school. I was very conscious of that fact. My family was supportive. They wanted me to go back to college, but I had chosen not to. I felt like I'd let them down. I wanted to find something that could make up for that and put me on a different path."

Whether it was heartbreak or something inside Joey telling him that he was destined for bigger things, he left Dalton and went on to serve in a variety of capacities within the marines. Eventually he became an explosive ordnance disposal (EOD) technician. His role as an EOD guy was the culmination of years of hard work and dedication that saw him consistently being recognized for his willingness to outwork everyone around him.

He served two combat deployments (one each in Iraq and Afghanistan) before losing both his legs in a 2010 IED-related incident.

Since his recovery and rehabilitation, he has worked in a variety of veterans affairs–related capacities. He is a 2016 graduate of Georgetown University. He has spoken with US presidents, members of the US Congress, high-ranking military officials, and cabinet officials. He also has found work as an actor, producer, and television news analyst.

Today he lives in a small town outside Atlanta with his family.

★★★

THE MISSION

We were in what we called the Green Zone—not the safe part of Iraq, but a strip of lush land along the Helmand River in Helmand Province, Afghanistan. We were there to push out the Taliban from the area so that we could get the farmers to stop growing poppies so that the Taliban wouldn't make any more money off of them. We were trying to make nice with the locals, the local shadow government who were mostly former mujahedeen fighters. So there was this kind of three-headed monster—the Taliban, the elected Afghan official, and their tribal or cultural leader.

The approach was this: Give the muj guy some money, provide him with a nice place to live, and get the local people to put their faith in him. He's going to be on our side. And in so doing, we'll passively push out the Taliban. The plan was working pretty well—really well, actually because money talks and bullshit walks. The locals didn't really trust us, but the muj guy had been around and he had their ear.

We were tasked with taking this target—Safar Bazaar, which was three to five miles outside the Green Zone. It was a trading town, a kind of walled city with a metal yard, and it was situated between the river and a canal. For the most part, US forces had left that town alone. The Taliban, noting that, covertly took it over. We had good intel, from drone footage, that the Taliban had left the area. So along with five other EOD techs and two hundred marines, we were going to clear it.

We encountered some resistance, and engaged in a few firefights on the way into Safar Bazaar. By the time we entered the walls of the city, there were no residents, no bad guys. It was like a ghost town, or at least felt like it.

Local accounts and drone footage pointed out what we thought was a hotel but was a kind of storage facility. That became our main objective. Drone footage showed bad guys pulling up to that location, staying for two or three days, and then leaving. Once we realized it was a storage building, we figured it was an even bigger problem. The first four and a half days, I cleared thirty-eight IEDs from the streets leading to the structure, not counting another dozen or so that were partially blown or were not yet fully armed. That was just with my team. Two other teams were also working that area.

At one point, we sent a team of green engineers to check out the structure itself. They came upon a few IED components they hadn't encountered before. One of those guys was a kid from Tennessee, Corporal Kristopher Daniel Greer, from Knoxville. He was a Volunteers fan. I used to kid him and say that I'd rather hang out with a Taliban dude than a Tennessee fan.

They called my teammate and me in. We confirmed that those components were unique. That meant that they needed to be reported quickly so other EOD techs could be made aware of this new threat and how it worked. For that, we needed to call in civilian counterparts who were there to gather forensic evidence. My teammate walked away to make that call.

We had cleared the area three times already. That was the rule. You checked it three times. If you found nothing, you called it clear.

So we had cleared it with metal detectors on foot three times. We thought it was safe.

NOT IF BUT WHEN

I stood up and put my protective gear back on. I took a step and was thrown, cartwheeling, in the air, the blast hitting me on my right side. When I landed, I was on my back.

I knew immediately what had happened. My lips were swelling and they felt like they were blown open from the inside out. I looked down and I could see my legs were gone, so I reached for my tourniquets. We kept them on our shoulders and our hips, because if we put them any lower on our limbs, they were probably going to get blown away with the limbs and we wouldn't have them when we need them.

The first place I reached was with my right arm up to my left shoulder to grab that tourniquet. My left arm was twisted around behind me, and when I pulled my right arm up, my right hand stayed in my lap, severed from the bones and the inside tissue on my right arm. I kind of just pulled my hand up into my belly and I thought, *Damn, I'm in a tight spot.* I kind of wiggled to get my left arm, and I couldn't feel it. I thought, *Well, I don't even know if I've got a left arm.* At that point I was like, *You know, I'm probably not making it out of this one.* I looked down past my legs, and I saw Daniel Greer lying down on his belly, looking back at me. His eyes were open, and he was either dead or passed out.

When Marines started coming to us, I had to kind of talk them in because I knew where the clear path was. When they got to me, they started working on me, and so I said, "Hey, man, say the Lord's Prayer with me." Because I just assumed, *Hey, if you're bleeding out two limbs, you ain't in good shape. If you're bleeding out three limbs, let's go ahead and call it a day.*

We got through it, and like we probably butchered that shit all to hell. And we just said it the best we could and we just basically said a prayer, and my eyes started swelling shut. And I remember one of them going, "We've got a heavy breather," talking about Greer. And I remember thinking, like in that moment, *What in the hell is a heavy breather? That's the dumbest thing I've ever heard. What does that even mean?*

So they carried him off. They came back and got me, carried me off. I stayed conscious until they got me into a mobile trauma bay, which is just basically a big sterilized box on the back of a truck that they can do field operations in. They got me in there. There was a female nurse, a corpsman that had been on that operation with us. I remember her talking to me a little bit. My eyes were swollen shut. And the next thing I knew, I woke up in the hospital in Germany two days later.

As soon as I woke up, this nurse pulled the tube out of my throat and they handed me a sponge to wet my lips. It took me a minute to be understood because I was so parched, and everything I said came out sort of cracky. The first thing I said was "Where's Greer?" She looked back at me and started going through her protocol. She's like, "You're in Landstuhl. You were hit by an IED. You lost both of your legs. You had severe damage to your arm, but we're going to be able to save it." And she goes, "Don't worry, honey. You're going to walk again."

And I remember two things. One, I remember believing her and never really questioning it after that. And two, I remember realizing I asked how Greer was and she told me I'm going to walk again. I asked, "But how's Greer?" She didn't say much. She left. About two hours later a doctor came in with a colonel, and they told me that Greer had suffered a head injury and was on life support, and his family were on the way there to take him off.

So I was awake for a day there. The next day they flew me back to DC.

LIFE CHANGES. "SO WHAT'S NEXT?"

You've got to understand, man. The number-one killers are bombs. The number-one thing that causes an amputee is a bomb. My entire life was playing with those bombs. It wasn't if but when, and how bad. That's something you accept before you get there, or you're not very good at the job. As a matter of fact, my teammate did not fully accept that reality before we got there. I ended up not getting along with him and ultimately did a lot of work by myself because I didn't trust him. Fear got too close. So that's just part of it. You can't blame him. Like, there's a reason why it's a volunteer job, and there's a reason why not a lot of people do it.

So, for me, you accept those things and you learn to accept them, and then you look past them. The moment I got hurt, it wasn't about, *Oh, shit, I lost my legs.* It was about, *Damn, am I going to live?* And then it was, *Okay, I'm alive. What am I going to do with it?* Like, *Tell me how prosthetics work. How long does it take until I can get on them? What can I do when I get on them? Has anybody ever run with them? Cool, I'm going to.* Like, that's just my personality. That's how I tackled it.

What I liked about being an EOD tech was I'd been in the war in Iraq before, so I had gotten that bug out, so it wasn't all about just chasing war glory. It was more about being productive and being a part of the effort. It was about being important and valuable and having an impact by that point.

What I also enjoyed about EOD was that our least important tool was our rifle. It wasn't about deciding who's good and who's bad or shooting somebody. It was about putting my life on the line to make life better for, most important, the other Americans there, but also the people that lived in the towns we were working in. You don't shit where you eat, so you don't put IEDs where you live. That's just not how it works. Like, the IEDs in the town we were in were not put there by the people that live there. And they were anxious to tell us about them because they were losing their kids to them, too. But they took a risk every time they did it, so we had to get creative on how they could tell us about them.

So you learn that, and then you have a vested interest, and the rest of it kind of goes away. Like, *Hey, this is my job*. Like, if my job is cleaning toilets, I'm going to have the cleanest toilets out there. If my job is taking apart bombs, by God, I'm taking apart these bombs. That's just the job at hand. There's a lot of pride in it, very much a lot of pride. I enjoyed the pats on the back. I'd be lying if I said I didn't. And I enjoyed the fact that if some shit's going to happen today, I know I'm going to be in it, nobody else, or I'll be the first one there.

A SHIFT IN PERSPECTIVE

There's a video clip from ABC's *Nightline* six days after I got hit. I said, "I don't look at this like I've lost my legs. I look at this like I've gained a second chance at life." To be honest, I don't know where that attitude came from. But if you can start there, which is pretty simple, you just build up and go forward. Losing my legs was the worst day of my life, simply because every day after that was better. Every day after that I was a little more healed, a little better for prosthetics, a little more experienced. I just wish people would take the time to appreciate the fact that we let so many things into our headspace and dictate if we're going to enjoy this moment or not that really should have no control over us. And you can use perspective to get there. Let's say you're sitting in a car and you know you're going to be late. It's five o'clock traffic, and you really wanted to be on time, but you know you're going to be late. You have a choice. You can spend however much time you have in traffic being pissed off and nervous about the fact that you're going to be late, or you can tune it to your favorite song, put it on your favorite temperature, and enjoy the fact that the worst thing about your life is something you can't even control, but you're comfortable and entertained.

That's just perspective. It's the same situation with relatively the same outcome. Don't make it worse. You might even make it better.

MAKING THE TRANSITION

I don't really miss being in the military. I miss being with the guys on my team. I had some goals for myself, but those had to change. What were going to be goals in rising in rank and responsibility in the marine corps changed to graduating from Georgetown. What was maybe going to be becoming a warrant officer and learning that side of the military became working on Capitol Hill. What used to be an adrenaline rush of *There's a bomb in front of me. I'd better take it apart* is now *Hey the green light came on, and I'm on live television. I better not say something stupid!*

You fill those gaps in your life with things that are equally fulfilling. And I think that's where a lot of veterans mess up. Your military service, no matter how long, is a chapter within your life's book, and too many veterans make it to the cover page and then don't know how to fill the rest of the pages. There's so much more to a human being than any one thing, and too many veterans make it so much a part of their identity, they don't know how to do something else or how to find fulfillment in doing something else.

And I know that finding that thing and then attaining that thing isn't easy. Too many people don't seem to get that today. I think that the old quote is, "Opportunity is often overlooked because it's dressed in overalls and looks a lot like work." A big problem we have right now in the age of information is that we can compare ourselves through social media to stories that aren't true, to highlight reels that don't show the negatives.

Some people would look at me five or six years after injury, where I'm running a nonprofit or going on television, and they would say, "You know, I was in the marine corps the same amount of time as you and I lost my legs. How do I get to do that?" And what they didn't see were the years where I did it for free. They didn't see the days where I went to therapy in the morning, worked on Capitol Hill during the day, and went to school at night. No matter where you are in life, wherever you want to be, that can be your goal, but it can't be your focus. Your focus has to be on the next task at hand. And that goes for anything.

If it's students graduating and wanting to go into a leadership position, if it's service members coming home and wanting to have a VA pension for the rest of their lives, whatever it is, focus on the task at hand. That's how you get to the goal. And what happens is sometimes even those tasks lead you in a different direction and there's a new goal you get to, and that's okay, too.

I think too often in the age of instant gratification and comfort, we overlook some really important, obvious things, which is that you can't get to tomorrow unless you live through today. And I think that's an important thing that a lot of us aren't focused on anymore.

The biggest problem veterans and others have is that it's no longer in their minds that coming home to small-town Iowa and running the one hardware store there is a life goal. Marrying the prom queen from small-town Iowa isn't a life goal. Now everyone seems to want something much bigger than that. Now you date coastal and your career is international and you're looking through this giant, broad window, and it's just hard to find fulfillment on the micro level. And that's what all millennials are doing. We're the first generation to have that big a window open for us, and it's kind of a fear of missing out. It's hard to accept *I can exist in this smaller microcosm and be fulfilled.* And I think that we're going to have to—it's a pendulum that's going to have to swing both ways.

Warrior cultures, like the Native American or ancient European, were societies that found a way to exist during war. You had to have warriors because you don't get to choose when you're at war. You are under attack. If it's this or that or the other, your society is susceptible to attack. A warrior puts on the armor, sharpens the sword, and stands guard, but most important, continues to live life to its fullest. It's not one or the other.

To be a warrior is to know that what you are involved in—life—is so precious and so important that you're willing to give yours so others can experience it. And that's it. Being a warrior is being a balance of things, not being just a fighter, not being just someone who wages war. I think that we lose that understanding sometimes. It's just as important to be a good dad as it is to be a good warrior. Otherwise, what are you fighting for? A warrior stays grounded and works hard.

If you want your marriage to work, put the work into it so that it's a strong marriage. If you want your career to work, put the work into it so that you're experienced and knowledgeable. Technology has led us to believe that there is an easy button that we can press. Maybe for some things, but not for the stuff that really matters. Not for the things that are going to last and that are going to outlast your time here on this planet.

CHAPTER 4

CAPTAIN (RET.)
CHAD FLEMING
UNITED STATES ARMY

After a while of feeling sorry for myself for losing my leg, I realized I was wasting time. I needed to find the good in the day.

I wanted to get back in the fight. My first deployment after I was injured was right back to Mosul—the same city where I had gotten blown up with two hand grenades and shot by an AK-47. So you talk about all of the different things running through your head. From the moment you're getting ready to leave the United States and you get on that aircraft and you realize, *Okay, when we land I'm going to get out in the city that when I left last time, I was on a gurney with all these machines hooked up to me, heading back to the United States.*

Then you land and they open that ramp and you smell the last smell that you smelled before you got on an aircraft to go to Balad, the next holding station—you can't describe that eerie, eerie feeling. But you have to push through. You have to push through, and I think that's maybe when you start becoming more of a warrior than actually the whole fighting piece and everything that you see in Hollywood and what Hollywood's description of a warrior is. When you go through those situations, when you continue to redeploy time after time after time, and all of those sensory things hit you when you land in a country where bad things have happened every time you've been there, and you can push through to complete your mission and get to that next objective, that's what starts creating a warrior. Because your other teammates, those new guys, they're looking at you as to what you are going to do.

So all of the subsequent times I went back over after sustaining injuries, I can't fully explain those feelings. And I think the easiest way to help someone understand that is, like in my case, every time I took a step, I had a constant reminder of what a bad day was. And if you think about it, a lot of people can't relate to that. Yeah, they've had bad days, but when you put on a prosthetic leg and you go back into a war zone and, every single step, when you go to bed at night and you take that leg off and you get up in the morning and you put that leg on, and you realize, *If I have a bad day, I could either repeat this injury and end up missing another leg or an arm, or I could die*, it's a totally different perspective on life and what combat is.

Because, especially for the type A, ego-driven person in those types of units, you don't ever think you can get injured. You deploy, you get in some bad situations, you come out okay. You go back; even worse situations, you come out okay. You start to create a sense of invincibility. You start to create a persona about yourself: *I'm either really good at what I do, sprinkled in with a little bit of luck or I'm just plain lucky and I'll take either one!* I'm surrounded by guys that are great at what they do. But you know what, whatever; I've got this safety blanket of *nothing's gone wrong, haven't been injured, haven't had to go home.* That can be a dangerous place to get into. I never got to that point because I had that constant reminder every single time I took a step. *This is what a bad day can be.*

★★

Captain Chad Fleming knows what a bad day can look like. While on deployment with the US Army's elite 75th Ranger Regiment in October 2005, he sustained injuries that would eventually cost him his leg. In some ways, it was due to the fact that Chad, who was a first lieutenant at the time, and his men were the *right* guys in the wrong place at the wrong time. He and his men were already scheduled to leave Mosul to get much-needed rest at the end of a deployment that saw them going out on more than 120 missions in a period of a hundred days. This was during the so-called surge in Iraq, when the operational tempo was high and the fighting intense; it was soon called the Second Battle of Mosul.

Prior to departing, Chad was working out in the gym when a call came in. Command had decided that because he and his squad were so familiar with the area of operation, they were going to be extended for a while longer. Intelligence had provided information that the number two bad guy in Iraq was in transit to a position within the city. He and another individual were considered high-value targets (HVT), and Chad and his men were selected to neutralize them.

Unlike most other missions for Special Operations, they went outside the wire in the middle of the day. Scorching 120-degree temperatures, full body armor, and the heat from their vehicle's engines all drenched them in sweat. Their mission set was to intercept the Iraqi's vehicle on a bridge. They navigated heavy traffic and arrived on site. They waited. They waited some more. Wondering if perhaps the intel was no longer good, they reached out to their command and were told to cross the bridge one last time in hope that their HVTs would arrive. At that point, Iraqi fighters ambushed the American vehicles and the men inside by dropping grenades from a highway overpass. One detonated inside the vehicle twelve to eighteen inches from Chad's position. They knew they had to exit the vehicle, and in the midst of the chaos came up with a plan to do that. Subsequently, the enemy forces engaged them in a firefight. During that, Chad was wounded in the upper thigh. The fighting was so fierce that the medics could not reach the wounded Rangers. Chad and his men performed self-aid and buddy-aid until they could be removed from the site.

As a result of those injuries, Chad had to endure twenty-three surgical procedures. He eventually became an amputee. He recovered from those wounds, and served five (!) additional deployments after rigorous, and successful, rehabilitation.

A native of Tuscaloosa, Alabama, Chad now resides outside Austin, Texas, where he lives with his wife and two children.

For his meritorious and valorous service to country, he has been awarded the Meritorious Service Medal, two Bronze Stars with Valor, and three Purple Hearts. Though he retired from active duty, he continues to serve our country and has remained active in the veterans' community. Despite his disability, he has completed running races, cycling races, Tough Mudders, and other endurance events. A sought-after public speaker, he continues to define what it means to be a warrior.

★★★★★★★★★★★★★★★★★★★★★★★★★★★★★★★★★★★★★★★

A HISTORY OF SERVICE

Chad wasn't the only member of his family to serve and to survive a bad day. His maternal grandfather, George Barry, served in the navy aboard the USS *Lexington* and survived its sinking. His father, Jack Fleming, served during the Vietnam War. Chad doesn't remember either man ever talking in any detail about their military careers, but somehow he got the message about the need to serve.

Growing up outside, playing army or playing soldier or whatever, I can remember back to when my family used to take vacations together. My cousins and my aunts and my uncles and all of us, even my grandparents, we'd all go down to the beach once a year. And I even remember when I was probably ten or eleven years old, the old airbrush place was down there. It used to be pretty popular. Everybody else was getting all this other stuff airbrushed, and I'd go in there and I'm like, "Hey, I want an army guy with a sniper hat, and I want it to say 'One Shot, One Kill' on it." So I had an airbrushed shirt when I was like eleven years old. I remember my cousins were like, "Dude, what are you thinking?" And I'm like, "This is what I'm going to do one day." And of course, everybody was telling me, "Okay, whatever." But I can remember that far back as to having that desire to serve in the military.

My dad's a huge history buff, and even watching movies with him and stuff, I remember way back when, one of my favorite movies used to be *The Big Red One* with Lee Marvin in it. I watched that movie as a kid, probably twenty-five times that I can remember. I can remember my dad saying, "Okay, I think you're old enough now, you can watch *Apocalypse Now*." And just watching all those movies with him I think kind of planted that seed as to, *Hey, this may be something you want to do*.

And I always had that type A personality. I was in athletics. I was always—I was very competitive, and I needed something that would challenge me. If I became bored in a sport, I would just not play that sport anymore. It had to be something that kept me engaged and moving. And I think that's what I saw in the military—no day's ever the same, it's always going to be different. Then if you go to a foreign country, if there's a war, if there's this, if there's that, there's always that challenge in the background waiting on you.

I was always drawn toward the Special Operations side. I remember watching *Rambo*. I'm like, "All right, what is he?" "Okay, well, he's supposed to be a Green Beret." "Okay, I got that." Then the movie *Navy SEALs* comes out with Charlie Sheen. "Okay, that's SEALs there. Okay." I can remember doing all my history work on *Okay, who's who?* So I developed the mindset that *I don't just want to be in the military. I want to go into the Special Operations community. I want the hard tasks, I want the hard jobs*. And that's what I set my mind to.

My dad had a different perspective because, obviously, the

Vietnam-era soldiers, airmen, marines, and sailors, they weren't involved in a popular war. My dad has always been extremely patriotic, and he's also been extremely supportive of everything that I've done. But when I came in and told him one day, "Hey, I'm about to go enlist," he was really kind of taken aback because I had a college degree. And he's like, "Son, at least if you're going to do this, go in as an officer." I'm like, "Dad, that's not what I want to do." I said, "I want to go in as an enlisted man and have some fun." So, of course, he gave me his perspective, and he was still supportive of my choice.

Later, when I was in college and working as a sheriff's deputy, a lot of people were kind of like, "You already have a job. Why are you looking to go and put yourself through basic training? You want to go in as an Airborne Ranger? Why would you do that at this age?" But it's the desire that I had, and I was hell-bent on making it work.

I went into law enforcement and did very well. I enjoyed helping people; I enjoyed just doing the job. But I had other aspirations, too. Military service was not only a way for me to get out and see the world, get out of that small town that I grew up in, but it was also an opportunity for me to go and do things that I had never done, and set my goals on something.

My parents also led by example with their work ethic. My mother was an accountant for General Motors. My dad was self-employed in the jewelry business. I saw the drive of both of them, and I think that's just kind of like, *Okay, what does that look like for me? I see what they do. Do I really want to do that? I don't know.* Because I worked for my dad. I started working for my dad when I was like thirteen years old. I was in a jewelry store, and a lot of people don't know this about me, but I have a master certification in jewelry fabrication. You hand me a torch and some platinum or some gold, I can make you just about anything you want. And I could do that when I was fifteen years old. I got a taste of the business world, and it just didn't light my fire. I think that's why I started looking into, *Okay, what else? What's going to keep me happy for the rest of my life?*

CHALLENGES AND OPPORTUNITIES

Chad was a Boy Scout, loved to hunt and fish, and was an outstanding high school football player who was recruited by several college and university programs.

In high school, I found a lot of success on the football field. I was lucky to be recruited by several college and university programs. I had an opportunity to play at the college level, and that was kind of when my first hardship in life reared its head. My mother was diagnosed with a terminal illness. And that changed everything. It changed all my plans. I wasn't mature enough to understand, really, at that time, what terminal illness meant. I think my immaturity was reflected in my belief that, *Okay, she's sick, but doctors can do just about anything. She's going to be okay.* And my mother was a very strong-willed person to begin with, and neither she nor my stepfather ever actually let me in on just how sick she was. There would be a couple of times that I would get a phone call: "Hey, can you go pick your mom up at work? She's too sick to drive home." "Yeah. Hey, Mom, you okay?" "Yeah, I just don't feel good today."

And that was the early days of when she was in what we now know as hospice. When they brought her home, she had a hospice nurse. This nurse is actually the one that told me. That was huge. I'm like, "Why is my mom home? She's doing good, right?" The nurse shook her head. "No, this is the final stages."

I thought, *Whoa, wait a minute. She's too young. This isn't supposed to happen to her.*

It threw me for quite a loop when my mother passed away, and it still, to this day, is on my mind all the time. I wonder what she would think of her grandkids. I know she would have been an awesome grandmother and all that kind of stuff. I think I struggled for a while because I also went through that *why me?* stage. I had plans. My plans were to go to college and do whatever it was I was going to do, and that abruptly got messed up when she passed away. I was bitter for a while.

Because of my mom's illness, I chose to stay home and attend junior college instead of attending college on a football scholarship. After my mother passed, I attended the University of Alabama during the day while also working the midnight shift as a Tuscaloosa County sheriff's deputy.

RANGER REGIMENT, THE REALITY OF COMBAT, AND WARRIORS

In the Special Operations community, you do a lot of hard training, and you always know that there may be a day when you have to put that training to work. But you don't know what that looks like until you get over there. And the thing is, through two different theaters—Afghanistan and Iraq—they were two very different wars. You were using a skill set in so many different ways, depending on what country you were fighting in.

You learn a lot about not only yourself, but about other people. So some people that you really looked up to at one point in time, when you see them under the stress of combat, you actually go back and question yourself: *Why was that person ever, at one point, so high on my list as a mentor or someone that I wanted to emulate? Because I just watched them basically fall apart during a combat operation.* And then you would see other people that you may not have ever looked at in that particular light, and they rise to the occasion, and you're like, *Wow, where did that come from?*

One of the biggest things that most service members will tell you is that they miss the fact that you truly learn about who your teammates are. And even when I speak now, I tell people one of the things that I miss the most about the military is that your teammates . . . you don't care what color they are. You don't care what church they go to. You don't care where they came from. You don't care who they love in life. You don't care anything about that. You care about, *Can you get me home? And, in turn, can I get you home?* That's the person to your right and to your left.

I can assure you, during the middle of a gunfight, you don't care what the person next to you looks like, and you don't care anything else about what they do. What you care about is, *This is my teammate. I'm going to get them home, or they're going to get me home.* And that's a bond that people don't understand if you haven't been in that situation. And you can't readily sit here and describe exactly how impactful or life-changing that bond is until you've had to go through it.

And you truly end up making friends for life that have that common bond. I can still tell you most of the key players that were on my team and where we were when it happened. Because you just put so much of your life and everything that's happening at that moment in someone else's hands. It gives you a true definition of what a teammate truly looks like, and I don't mean looks like from a physical standpoint, but from a mental standpoint, and what that person's made of.

I watched a documentary show that tried to answer this question: Is there such a thing as a warrior gene? They took MMA fighters, they took professional football players, they took all these people that people sometimes label "hero" or "warrior" or "tough guy." They pulled some guys out of the Special Operations community, as well as other parts of the military, and said, "Is there truly this warrior gene out there?"

The conclusion was that none of the MMA fighters that they tested had the so-called warrior gene. They just happened to be good athletes who were very proficient at their particular sport and were considered professional at what they did. If you'd take that person and drop them into the middle of Iraq or Afghanistan and say, "Okay, now you have to go fight and actually prove that you're a warrior," the answer was no. The same was true with most of the other athletes.

The only ones that had the warrior gene came out of the Special Operations community. Two of the major determiners were resilience and the ability to compartmentalize. Because if you can't compartmentalize things, and that teammate to your right or to your left gets killed, and then you can no longer function, you're either going to get killed as well or you're going to get somebody else killed. And as traumatic as it might be with that person to your right or to your left, or one of your best friends, that you realize is no longer with you, can you continue and complete the mission? Your opportunity to mourn is going to have to take place at a later time.

I've seen so many guys, so many impressive guys, that really rose to the challenge. I have numerous friends that have been awarded medals for valor, including Medal of Honor recipients. And when you talk to some of those guys, they're like, "Hey, man, I didn't do anything that we all haven't done." You know, we rise to the occasion. We rise to the highest level of training that we have. And when you're scared and you're fighting for your life, you can do things that you wouldn't normally do. I'm not saying that to take away anything from others that have done heroic things. Warriors always have that in them. A warrior will always rise to the occasion and give everything they have to complete the mission and save their friends' lives, save their lives, and move on to the next objective.

SETTING THE RIGHT EXAMPLE

After you get injured, you're immediately separated from your team and those people that you care about the most. They go on, and they're living their lives. You have to open a new chapter in your life, which is going to make you different than everybody else. Your desire to go back and be with them will never wane. I can remember being on the aircraft flying from Landstuhl, Germany, to Walter Reed, going, "When can I get back with the guys?" And all through that hardship, the fight was to get back with the guys. I almost felt as if I was letting them down because I wasn't there.

Then I realized, *Okay, I survived this.* This is making me stronger. Now I can go back and teach some of those other guys, maybe things to do, things not to do, maybe something that will keep you alive or maybe just the visual impact of, *Hey, we know what happened to this guy, and he's right here with us again. So you know what? If he can continue doing what he's doing with one good leg, then I'm going to continue doing what I'm doing.*

There may be a warrior gene, but I don't think there's a persistence gene. Some people never have to face a real test in their lives. I don't know if I was a real persistent person until I lost my leg. I thought I was, but I don't know if I was really at my peak persistence and perseverance level.

Sure, I gave 100 percent effort. I didn't quit. But now that gets compounded and magnified when you're doing that outside of your comfort zone. You take someone with an injury, you take someone with a physical disability, you take someone with a mental disability, and that person goes, *You know what? I am not going to quit until I achieve my goal, no matter what.* I think that's learned.

My ten-year-old son and I were working cattle, just two days ago, and we were having to string fence. And I said, "Hey, buddy, you've got to cross that creek right there, carrying this cable, and you have to go over there and hook it on that fence." And he gets across the creek, and the far bank is pretty steep and muddy. Three tries later, he tells me that he can't do it. "Don't ever tell me you can't do something, son." And I didn't lose my mind, but I went into that whole, "Hey, son, don't ever use the word 'can't!' If I can come over there and I can climb that hill with one good leg, then you can get up that hill."

He turned right around, back toward that bank, and he scampered up that hill, and he hooked that cable on the fence just like I told him to do.

I kind of sat back, and I was like, I remember my dad telling me, "Don't ever say the word 'can't,' son. You can always figure out a way around it." And you're just kind of like, *Yeah, okay, whatever.* But looking at me that day when I told him that and it registered with him, *You know what? My dad's got a point. He can get over here and he can climb this hill. Why can't I?* And he literally got up there in a heartbeat.

I tend to think that I have a different outlook on what the words "persistence" and "perseverance" actually mean, and it's because of—call it what it is—it's because of my disability. And my disability, I will never let it hold me back. I'll figure out how to make something work and I will continue to drive on until it either crushes me or it kills me, because that's what drives me. That's the person that I am.

I'm kind of known in the veteran community for saying things like it is, and a lot of times it's not popular. But I can say it because I'm a disabled veteran. So what are you going to do? Are you going to tell me that I'm heartless and I don't understand how you feel? Wrong answer, buddy! I'm not a starfish. This leg ain't going to grow back, so guess what: I know what you're going through. You can be a victim only if you allow yourself to be a victim. And I think that's what irritates me the most about veterans that allow themselves to play the victim. There is so much money, there is so much help, there are so many benevolent organizations out there that are screaming, "Let us help you. Let us do something for you," that in my opinion, there's no reason for you to be a victim. If you choose to allow yourself to be a victim, then you're part of the problem.

For veterans there's money here for this, there's money there for that, there's all these things that can help you get back to being the person that you were and help you figure out your next chapter in life. My motto for life has been, "Not every day's a good day, but there's good in every day." And when I realized that, I was recovering from being an amputee, and I was feeling sorry for myself. *Man, why me?* All of this stuff, and I could find every reason to tell myself why I could no longer succeed.

Hell, the good in a day can be that I woke up and took a freakin' breath. That's a good day right there. And then if you're surrounding yourself with people that are good for you and that believe in you and want to help you, then there's the rest of the good in the day.

There's nothing I can't do with this prosthetic leg—nothing. With technology and everything else and the desire to do what you want to do, they'll make a leg for you to do whatever you want—I've got fourteen legs in my closet right now. I can do anything from climb a mountain, to swim, to ride a bicycle, to live in Texas and put on my boot leg because I love my cowboy boots. So they had to make me a leg just so I can wear cowboy boots.

Don't say that it can't be done. It can.

Fighting a war, there's nothing pretty
about it. Your heart and your warrior spirit
take you over there to do the job.

—*Captain Chad Fleming*

★

Military service is a way of life. We follow a code.

—*Captain Sean Parnell*

★

I feel like a patriot now, not just because I
was able to serve, but because I have such a
deep appreciation for the way we live.

—*Lieutenant Commander Caroline Johnson*

★

That's the reality of combat; it doesn't care.
No bullet has your name on it.
The bullets say, "To whom it may concern."

—*Jocko Willinik*

PART II

BEARING
WITNESS

I served alongside some heroes, and I
was honored to be there with them.

—*Sergeant Major Eric Geressy*

★

I think about the time I spent with my kids,
sharing stories of the amazing heroes I served
with. I hope that they'll aspire to be like them.

—*Lieutenant Colonel Scott Mann*

CHAPTER 5

SERGEANT MAJOR (RET.) ERIC JOSEPH GERESSY

UNITED STATES ARMY

I don't like talking about myself. Everything we did was a team effort, and all did their part. There were many sacrifices made in Iraq, more than anyone knows, and we must never forget. I had the honor to serve alongside some real heroes. I was honored to be there with them. I am their witness.

In September 2007, at the tail end of the Iraq troop surge, I was the first sergeant for Eagle Company, 2nd Squadron, 2nd Stryker Cavalry Regiment. The company was assigned to occupy and conduct operations out of Combat Outpost Blackfoot (COP Blackfoot) in East Rashid, southern Baghdad. The sector, plagued with Sunni and Shia sectarian violence, was the last al-Qaeda stronghold in Baghdad.

This was a very dangerous sector: al-Qaeda in Iraq controlled one side of the street, Jaysh al-Mahdi (Mahdi militia) controlled the other, and COP Blackfoot sat in the middle. This sector was known as al-Qaeda's Castle—the center for its leadership. So it was Sunni Iraqis against the Shia Iraqi government and the US forces.

After doing a brief recon assessment of the area, I reported back into our squadron commander, Colonel Myron Reineke. He was a leader I held in high regard.

Colonel Reineke asked me how the recon went.

"Sir, we won't have any trouble finding the enemy."

"What do you mean?"

"Well, apparently, they're right at the gates of the outpost. Parts of a blown-up Stryker are two hundred meters from the entry control point. The outpost defense also needs to be improved. They have taken several casualties in and around the outpost, and it does not look like any improvements had been made recently. I am sure we will not have any trouble finding the enemy."

Two things needed to be done. First, we would establish the defense of COP Blackfoot. Second, we would take the fight directly to the enemy. I had a feeling before we moved out there that we would not have a lot of time before the enemy tested us. This being my third tour of duty in Iraq, I also knew that the enemy would take advantage of the new units as they rotated into country. I would be proven right in the next several days.

★★

As a first sergeant, Eric Geressy received the Silver Star, the army's third-highest personal decoration for valor in combat, as a result of his actions on September 4, 2007, during Operation Iraqi Freedom. He was recognized for "his outstanding leadership, tactical astuteness, flawless performance under enemy fire that brought devastating effects upon the enemy and kept his soldiers alive during the defense of COP BLACKFOOT."

Born in Staten Island, New York City, Eric grew up in the South Beach section, a predominately Irish and Italian community where many police officers and firefighters made their homes—including his father, who was a mechanic servicing the vehicles used for the New York Police Department commissioner. Eric knew from an early age that he wanted to serve his country in a different role— as a soldier. He was influenced by a family tradition of service to the country. His paternal grandfather, Sigmund Geressy, served with the army's 71st Infantry in World War II. His "adopted" grandfather, Mitch Rech, made three combat parachute jumps in Sicily, Salerno, and Nijmegen while serving with the army's 82nd Airborne Division—a unit which Eric eventually was part of. Another great-uncle, a Silver Star recipient, lost his life in World War II while serving with the Office of Strategic Services (OSS), the precursor of the Central Intelligence Agency. Technical Sergeant Rosario Squatrito and several other members of his unit were executed after being captured during Operation Ginny, their mission to destroy a railway tunnel that would cut the lines of communications for all German forces in central Italy. That execution was in violation of the terms of the Geneva Convention, and eventually the perpetrators were among the first to be tried for war crimes. The German commander for all forces in the Mediterranean, General Albert Kesselring, would be sentenced to death, and his war crimes trial became the model for the Nuremberg trials. Much of this was unknown to the family for years.

Eric also came under the influence of his uncle, Tom Rockett, who also served in two branches of the military, first as a member of the Coast Guard serving on the USCGC *Barataria*, where he received a commendation for participating in the rescue of four sailors who went overboard from a US Navy ship in 1959. He later enlisted into the army and became a Special Forces weapons sergeant with Charlie Company, 3rd Battalion, 20th Special Forces Group. Eric was a self-described "mess in school who only went on to earn a GED for the sole purpose to join the military." With instructions from his uncle, Eric went to the recruiter's office and told them he wanted to enlist for the Airborne Infantry. After taking the preliminary aptitude test, which indicated he was a prize recruit, Eric had different options in various military occupational skills to choose from, but he was set on being an infantryman.

As a seventeen-year-old private serving along the Korean border, he fell under the spell of a platoon sergeant, a squad leader, and a first sergeant who had all served with distinction in the Vietnam War. They were hard-nosed, no-nonsense types who showed Eric the right way through example and shared stories of Hamburger Hill, LZ X-ray, Army Rangers, and the 1st Cavalry. Eric would eventually put some of those lessons on the importance of the basics and attention to detail to good use in his tours during the global War on Terror.

Eleven years later Eric was stationed with the 25th Infantry Division in Schofield Barracks, Hawaii, and was there during the September 11, 2001, attacks on our country.

He received a call in the middle of the night about what was taking place in New York, but it took days for him to find out what had happened to his mother, father, and aunt, who all worked in Manhattan at the time—they were all uninjured. After these events Eric wanted to do his part in what he believed would be the response to these attacks. This was just not an attack on the country; this was an attack on his home.

Eric Geressy served with distinction in the 3rd Brigade, 101st Airborne Division's Rakkasans. He also was a platoon sergeant in Bravo Company, 2nd Battalion, 187th Infantry (Air Assault) during the invasion of Iraq in 2003–2004. Upon return from that deployment, after thirteen months he was promoted to company first sergeant for Charlie Company, 3rd Battalion, 187th Infantry (Air Assault), serving in Iraq in 2005–2006. During this time, yours truly—Pete Hegseth—served with First Sergeant Geressy in both Baghdad and Samarra, Iraq.

His third combat deployment to Iraq was just four months after returning from the past deployment. This time he was serving as the Eagle Company, 2nd Squadron, 2nd Stryker Cavalry Regiment first sergeant.

After three deployments he was awarded the Combat Infantryman Badge, the Army Commendation Medal with Valor, three Bronze Stars, the Silver Star, and was recommended for the Distinguished Service Cross by General Raymond Odierno. The DSC was approved by General David Petraeus, but even after two four-star generals in command on the ground in Iraq recommended and approved the DSC recommendation, for unknown reasons the medal was never awarded. Today he continues to serve the country in his capacity as a Department of Defense contractor.

★★

FIRST THINGS FIRST—AND FAST

While our first rifle platoon moved out to COP Blackfoot, I stayed back at FOB Falcon with about thirty junior enlisted soldiers and maybe two sergeants to do the last preparations required for the Stryker vehicles to conduct combat operations.

Adding RPG cages to the Strykers, and several other parts, required these young soldiers to really work hard. They went at it and got all the additions completed very quickly in about two days. While this was going on, I noticed that there was a stockpile of bulletproof glass, what the troops called "pope glass." After the recon at Blackfoot, I felt we could use this bulletproof glass in the construction of the bunkers we would build on the roof of COP Blackfoot. We loaded as much of this as we could into our Stryker vehicles before departing from the FOB to COP Blackfoot.

Once I got on the ground at the COP, the company commander and several others went back to the FOB, leaving me as the only company-level leader at the outpost. I did a walk-around. Then I got all the platoon leaders and platoon sergeants together. At the time several members of the company were focused on the sleeping quarters for the platoons. That was the last thing on my list of priorities. At this meeting I put out the company priorities of work. That is the first thing you're supposed to do when establishing a company defense position. I told them we would figure out the sleeping situation once we finished improving the fighting positions and defensive plan for the outpost. This is as back to the basics as you can get when it comes to infantry tactics.

We sandbagged all the windows, which was backbreaking work for the troops, especially since we laid them lengthwise—that way the bullets had a longer path to travel. As a result, we used about triple the number for better protection, and had to haul them by hand up sets of stairs. We also built rooftop bunkers and prepositioned additional ammunition, medical bags, and litters (stretchers) at the top of the four stairwells to have easy access in case we needed them quickly. Our company mortar section was led by Staff Sergeant Elvin Yazzie, a Native American from the Navajo Nation, who was a true, quiet professional.

He established a firing point on the roof of the outpost with a 60 mm mortar system to include a sandbagged ammunition storage area for the 60 mm mortars. I also quickly requested 50 caliber machine guns and MK-19 grenade launchers from our squadron headquarters company, and they were placed into operation just a few hours before the attack began. So far, so good, with everyone pulling their weight.

The final part of the construction of the defense was erecting a camouflage net that covered the entire rooftop of the outpost. We did this at night with most of the soldiers wearing night vision goggles. During this last addition, I heard a lot of grumbling and cursing as the troopers set this up. They had been working nonstop, some for forty-eight hours, some for seventy-two, to fortify that building. We were running those young troopers ragged, and I could imagine what the enemy was thinking, hearing all the construction sounds.

Once everything was set in place, we conducted several rehearsals on how we would fight the defense of the combat outpost. We went over what each platoon would do if we were attacked, who would man the primary and alternate fighting position, how we would reinforce the troops on the roof in case of contact, how to respond and evacuate casualties if we had them. We went over every contingency, preparing for the worst. We completed these rehearsals and were all set by the night of September 3, 2007.

EXPERIENCES TEACH YOUR GUT

Every action I took and each decision I made on September 4, 2007, was based on my training, education, and experience. I learned so much in my previous two combat deployments to Iraq. I felt I understood the enemy tactics and the nature of the fight. My number one priority was to get everyone back home safely to their families and to complete the mission. I defined mission success as all assigned objectives from our higher headquarters being accomplished and getting everyone involved in the operation back safely. When I received the radio call from the TOC to send a patrol out to look for the vehicle-borne improvised explosive device (VBIED), I was hesitant because I had served in this part of Baghdad in 2005. I understood the enemy tactics used in that location. I suspected this was a baited ambush, and therefore I delayed sending out that patrol.

Another consideration I had was that we had just gotten there and were unfamiliar with the sector either in daylight or at night. Also, the tip came from an unknown source. It could easily be a setup. Going out, dismounted, looking for a car bomb was dangerous business anytime, and I wanted to make sure if we had to do this, we had the tactical advantage. This discussion went back and forth with the TOC for hours, well into the next afternoon, until finally we were directed to execute the patrol. I gave a final objection on the radio, but then told them we would execute, and then finalized the plan to do so.

Sticking to the basics, our company-level planning always consisted of a warning order, operations order, concept of the operation, and back brief. Then came what I felt was an important part of planning, the rehearsal of concept drill (ROC drill); we did this for every operation. During the ROC drill we had each tactical level leader talk their part of the operation from the movement into the objective area, the cordon, assault, and the withdrawal off the objective.

This allowed every element leader to understand the overall concept of the operation. It also allowed us to discuss, as a group, any contingency. In every plan the enemy gets a vote, so you have to develop courses of actions to deal with things that could go wrong with the initial plan.

By delaying sending the patrol until the next day, we had the element of surprise on the enemy. The units we replaced at the outpost went into sector only at night, so when we conducted this patrol in the middle of the day, the enemy was completely caught off guard and not prepared to react. The patrol would be conducted by 3rd Platoon, led by First Lieutenant Chris Turner and his platoon sergeant, Staff Sergeant Jeremy Hare. I directed 2nd Platoon, led by First Lieutenant Jim Weber and Staff Sergeant Brian Glynn, as COP security manning the fighting positions on the COP defense; and 1st Platoon was led by First Lieutenant Fernando Pelayo with Sergeant First Class Raymond Bittinger as his platoon sergeant leading the quick reaction force. They would be loaded into the Strykers, ready to roll out in case we needed to reinforce 3rd Platoon or conduct casualty evacuation (CASEVAC) while in contact with the enemy. Everyone else would be ready at COP Blackfoot. I also had requested an aerial weapons team to be on station in order to provide overwatch and support to 3rd Platoon. Members of the 1st Cavalry Division dismounted two AH-64 Apache attack helicopters to the suspected vehicle-borne improvised explosive device.

All that preparation paid off. They came under attack, killed three enemy fighters, and sustained no friendly casualties. The battle had just begun, however.

THIS WAS NO DRESS REHEARSAL

Soon after conducting an after action review, checking on some troops who were heat casualties from the daylight operation in 120- to 130-degree temperatures, the outpost came under attack. The enemy fired on the COP with mortars, machine guns, sniper rifles, and rocket propelled grenades. They had massed on the outpost from three different directions and were firing from some buildings that allowed them to fire down onto our positions.

When the platoons were manning their fighting positions, I was preparing to move to the rooftop. As I was doing this, I could hear screams for a medic. As the attack started, Specialist Ryan Holley was standing up behind his M240B machine gun when he was shot in his shoulder between his body armor plates. The sniper's bullet went right through his body and came out of his back, with the round hitting and sticking out of one of the M203 grenade rounds he was carrying. Somebody reacted quickly and tossed that grenade over the side.

When I got on the roof, I immediately started to yell for the company to increase the amount of fire onto the enemy so we could gain fire superiority. At the same time I saw Holley lying in a pool of blood screaming. I joined two other soldiers in assisting him. Someone spotted a grenade and threw it off the roof.

With so much gunfire, explosions, and screaming, it was a very chaotic moment. We got Holley onto the litter. I carried the front and sniper Specialist Tamim Fares had the back. We moved back into the stairwell then down the stairs. Halfway, we were met by Captain Benjamin Blanks, our doc, and several of his medics. They took Holley to the aid station.

Back on the roof, I moved from position to position trying to assess what the enemy was doing and to encourage our soldiers.

I remember saying to a few of them, "We are doing good!" But at that stage I wasn't so sure of that. After making it around the roof I was going back up and down the stairs to the company command post to use the radio to provide situation reports to our squadron commander, as well as direct the firing of the attack helicopter. During the fight this went on for several hours.

One of the key preparations we did prior to the attack was putting up the camouflage net. I am not sure who came up with the idea. I think it was Staff Sergeant Darryl Card, who was a squad leader in 3rd Platoon at the time. I knew we had to put something up to camouflage the fighting positions on the roof somehow. But my NCOs figured it out and got the net set up, covering up the entire roof over every fighting position. This really made a big impact on the outcome of the fight because it caused the enemy to shoot high over the positions. This helped as we ran around moving from position to position during the fighting. The enemy shot at the netting so much it had been lit on fire in a few spots.

Early in the fighting we pinpointed one of the enemy machine gun locations that was firing down onto the COP. I felt this was the first enemy position that needed to be destroyed. I went through the call for fire request with the helicopters supporting us. When making this call one of the main elements is marking the enemy positions. We normally would have used tracer rounds from our machine guns in the day, but there was so much fire going back and forth between us and the enemy that the pilots could not confirm the enemy position. I then directed one of our snipers to fire a few smoke grenades on the suspected enemy machine gun position. Once we did this, the pilots were able to confirm the enemy location, and I cleared them hot on the engagement using Hellfire missiles.

After their first shot we stood there watching it going toward the target for a while, but then it suddenly went hard left into a nearby house. Seeing that happen was like a punch in the gut. No one wants there to be civilian casualties, and we all did our best to prevent things like that from happening. Since I was the one who called it in, I felt immediately responsible for the errant missile.

A few moments later, the pilot called me on the radio and reported that it was a missile malfunction. We went through the call for fire process again and I cleared him hot on the target. They placed two Hellfire missiles into the position, silencing the enemy machine gun for the rest of the battle.

The following day our squadron sent out another company to conduct a battle damage assessment of where the errant missile had impacted. The unit reported back that the house was not filled with civilians. It had been the location of the enemy mortar system that was firing onto COP Blackfoot, supporting the enemy attack. They also discovered three dead enemy fighters at the location with the destroyed mortar, and found several AK-47s. I am not sure what the chances are of that happening, but I think God was really looking out for us that day.

QUIET HEROISM

When Eric received his citation for the Silver Star in January 2008 for his conduct during that attack on COP Blackfoot, it stated that they had taken on 35 to 45 "determined enemy fighters." Later intelligence revealed that as many as 200 to 250 enemy combatants participated in the attack. The US victory was the beginning of the end for al-Qaeda in that sector. The battle that took place on September 4 was just the beginning for Eagle Company. From that point on they went out on the offensive, and there were many rough days ahead of clearing house to house. They, along with the 3rd Squadron of the 2nd Stryker Cavalry Regiment who assisted them, encountered more than two hundred IEDs that had to be removed by the EOD teams. 3/2 SCR lost six soldiers KIA on two consecutive days to house-borne IEDs.

During one of those house-clearing operations, Staff Sergeant Card was blown into the street and had shrapnel all through his backside and legs when an IED detonated. He also lost his hearing for quite a bit. He got up, brushed himself off, and continued to lead his squad into the building they were consolidating in. Unfortunately, Specialist Jonathan Pruziner lost his left leg below the knee in that blast, which also wounded several other soldiers from the squad.

As soon as the Strykers dropped their ramps to dismount and load up the wounded, the enemy increased their fire from the rooftops and windows. As the soldiers were returning fire and getting behind cover, one soldier, Private First Class Tom Morris, stood fearlessly in the middle of the street, returning fire. That suppressed the enemy fire enough so that Specialist Pruziner could be loaded into the Stryker. During the evacuation, enemy fighters disembarked from a vehicle. They were emplacing an IED, hoping to target one of our CASEEVAC vehicles. They'd seen that same vehicle and crew assisting a different casualty earlier on. I cleared the AH-64 hot, and they engaged the enemy, detonating that IED and taking out the three enemy fighters in the process.

Despite the toll being taken on us, we never lost our humanity. Several days after Staff Sergeant Card and Specialist Pruziner and the others were wounded, we were in another firefight. From the rooftop, I could see a man running with something in his arms. Suspiciously, the enemy stopped firing. The man came nearer, and we could see he was carrying a child. Our soldiers searched him in case he was a suicide bomber. I rushed down the stairs and out there to join a few of the other guys who were bringing out a litter.

Once the boy was loaded up, we carried him toward the entrance of the COP. As we were running, I noticed there was something strange about the soldier in front of me. He was wearing all his gear, body armor, helmet, but did not have any boots. Instead, he was wearing flip-flops. I then realized it was Staff Sergeant Card. When we got the kid back to our aid station for Captain Blanks to work on, I asked Staff Sergeant Card, "What the hell are you doing out there running around with us? You were just wounded and your legs and feet are so swollen you can't fit them into your boots."

His response was, "Well, I saw you guys going out there and I could not just sit around doing nothing; I had to help."

This selfless action sums up how the members of Eagle Company conducted themselves every day, and shows what they were made of. America can be extremely proud of how these young soldiers represented our country during some exceedingly difficult days.

We fought some really bad people in Iraq, and we were the only ones there that could do anything about what they were doing to the Iraqi people and to the rest of the coalition forces. I am humbled and honored to have served alongside our nation's bravest, best, and brightest. At the end of the deployment, 2nd Squadron, 2nd Stryker, Cavalry Regiment was awarded the Valorous Unit Award, the equivalent of the entire unit receiving the Silver Star. Each soldier of the unit will wear that ribbon for the rest of their time in the army, and new soldiers serving in the unit will wear it when they are part of the unit as a reminder of those that went before them. America can be proud of how these service members conducted themselves and brought honor to our country.

Eugene Sledge, in *With the Old Breed: At Peleliu and Okinawa*, said it best: "War is brutish, inglorious, and a terrible waste. . . . The only redeeming factors were my comrades' incredible bravery and their devotion to each other. Marine Corps training taught us to kill efficiently and to try to survive. But it also taught us loyalty to each other—and love. That esprit de corps sustained us."

CHAPTER 6

SERGEANT
MAT BEST
UNITED STATES ARMY

I was so inspired to learn
that there were these groups
of people who were trained
killers that could handle any
situation, but they led with
empathy and compassion.

The percussive effects of our door breach and the sparking illumination of the flash bang had just settled when my teammate Hansen and I entered the main ground-floor room of a traditional Iraqi home. Across from us, a set of stairs angled upward. Flanking it were two closed doors. Hansen and I headed for the door on the right; Sergeant Dale G. Brehm and my squad leader, Sergeant Ricardo Barraza—both of them legends among Army Rangers—took the one to the left. We breached our door and saw nothing.

"Clear," we shouted simultaneously.

The sound of rapidly stuttering gunfire reached us. It took a moment for it to fully register. The sound was coming from the room next door.

"I'm hit. I can't move."

I recognized Brehm's voice.

I was nineteen at the time and Brehm was twenty-three. I'd been with him on my first deployment. Now we were together again on our second. I'd not seen any real combat action our first go-around. I was eager to experience it. Brehm had been my tutor, another older brother who showed me the ropes, made me want to be a better Best.

Not hesitating, knowing that I was putting myself in line of sight of whoever had shot my hero, I busted ass into the room. I spotted two human shapes on the floor. One large and one small. Adrenaline pumping even more than before, I dragged the closest, the smaller of the two bodies, Brehm's, back into the main room. I checked him out, lifting up pieces of his body armor. I couldn't see any wounds.

Unsure of what to do next, I was startled by a viscous sound. Blood bubbled past Brehm's lips and down both sides of his face.

Curses spewed out of my mouth. I gathered myself and did what Brehm had instructed me to do. I got on the radio and called in a medic. I knelt over Brehm, still not sure what had happened and what else was going on all around us.

★★

Veteran of five combat deployments and four hundred direct action confrontations. YouTube comedy pioneer. Entrepreneur. High school emo band and botany club member. Army Ranger. Son of a marine. Youngest brother of two marines who served in Iraq. *New York Times* bestselling author.

Mat Best defies easy categorization. Regardless of that, his mission is clear: to inform, to inspire, and to entertain.

Born in Santa Barbara, California, into a family with a rich tradition of military service, Mat knew at an early age what he wanted to do with his life. He had a number of cousins who became Navy SEALs. "I was about eight and went to an aunt's house with my dad for a visit. In walked these jacked, chiseled men in their BDUs. They were nice enough to bring along some equipment to show me, including night vision goggles. I looked through them and saw these American badasses and knew I wanted to be like them. That visit changed the course of my entire life."

Heavily influenced by the film *Black Hawk Down*, and eager to best his brothers and forge his own path, at seventeen, Mat chose to enlist in the army. His goal was to become a Ranger—a member of the elite light infantry combat formation. He remembers seeing his brothers Alan and Davis graduating from US Marine boot camp—on September 11, 2001. The moment was made even more poignant due to the fact that Alan was also informed that day of a Hodgkin's lymphoma diagnosis. Mat always looked up to his brothers, while also trying to outdo them, but how he saw Alan deal with that bad news continues to inspire him. Alan's stoicism in the face of a disease that could potentially derail his dreams (and stoicism in the face of his brother's relentless teasing about his condition), and his efforts to overcome the debilitating effects of his treatment, and his ability to scheme in order to be deployed along with Davis to Iraq, left an indelible impression on Mat.

Mat inspires the same in others. He is dedicated to helping veterans. His latest post-service venture is the Black Rifle Coffee Company. It is a veteran-owned organization whose stated objective is to employ veterans and to serve fine coffee to those who love America.

★★★★★★★★★★★★★★★★★★★★★★★★★★★★★★★★★★

While the medics tended to our two fallen leaders, we still had work to do. We checked another room and found a bad guy with an AK-47. Before he had a chance to fire at us, we took him out. He lay there, and all I could see were Brehm's and Barraza's inert bodies. I took out my anger on the dude's face, pummeling him with my fists. The only regret I had was that he couldn't feel the punishment I was raining down on him.

I was even angrier a few minutes after we helped load Brehm and then Barraza into the first of several medevac helos. No sooner had the second one's wheels left the ground than a huge explosion lit up the night sky. Later we learned that a fourteen-year-old kid was hiding out in an armoire in the same room where Brehm and Barraza had taken rounds. Little shit detonated his suicide vest while our guys were standing there reluctant to take a kid out and offering him a chance to surrender. Three of our guys and one SEAL team member paid the price of that, with ball bearings impacting and entering their bodies. Fortunately, they all survived their serious injuries.

We mopped up and got back inside the wire after 6 a.m. That's when we found out that Brehm and Barraza had been killed in action. I was able to go stateside for Brehm's burial at Arlington National Cemetery. I remembered a conversation I'd had with Dale during that second deployment: "Hey," he said, "if I ever go down, you'd better use my radio and take control. If there's one thing I'm going to do, it's get you home to your family, even if it means I have to die." That's always weighed on my soul, because that's what he did. He went into the room with Barraza, got in a gunfight, and essentially saved my life.

THE HARSHEST REALITY

Later, when I became a team leader, I communicated that same ideal to my team: "Guys, I'm going to be the first one through the door. If I die, then your job is to fuckin' live."

I wanted them, the younger guys, to experience as much as they could in life. I was pretty convinced that I was—not to be a martyr—going to die during my last deployment. The operational tempo was so fast during that last stretch, I didn't see any way that couldn't happen. Either that, or I was going to be seriously wounded. Nearly one-third of my platoon had or would receive a Purple Heart for being wounded.

I realized later, in talking to army buddies and guys we hired at Black Rifle Coffee, that all of them at some point had come to the same conclusion. Most of us wrote "the letter" to our parents and gave it to a buddy to deliver to them after we died. That sounds like it's something out of a movie, but it's not. It's real. That letter exists. In it I told my mom and my dad that I loved them, and I thanked my brothers for everything they did.

Two months later, I got out. I was alive and I counted all my fingers and toes and limbs and they were all there. Looking ahead, I had no idea what I was going to do with my life. Looking behind, I was damn proud of what we'd all done. Still, it was strange to think that at that point in my career, I was like, *Okay, I'm going to die. Screw it. I'll do the best job I can and bring as many of my teammates home as I can.* I was a team leader. That's what you were supposed to do, just like Brehm and Barraza had.

As is true for many returning combat veterans, Mat's transition to civilian life was not easy. He experienced a near idyllic childhood and adolescence in and around Santa Barbara. As the youngest of six, he enjoyed the privilege of having parents who were somewhat depleted by the experience of overseeing his older siblings. He reveled in the independence his brothers had earned for him. He spent long days on his BMX bike; fished for hours off Stearns Wharf; and spent overnights in the mountains of New Cuyama with his brother Alan, with nothing more than a .22, a shotgun, a couple of old military MREs from his dad's cache, and a sleeping bag. His sense of adventure had spurred his desire to work in Special Operations. He enjoyed the bonds he formed, and doubted if he'd ever experience that kind of loyalty and sense of purpose again. He'd joined the army with a romantic notion of war and combat. As he said, "I thought war was cool. I could serve my country and do all this cool stuff. Even after my first deployment, I still felt that way. I didn't realize the severity of war, the complications and implications of going in and getting into a gunfight."

Losing his team leader and squad leader forced him to understand that the stakes are, as he put it, "insanely high."

Part of his difficulty in transitioning had to do with understanding better who he was and how he'd evolved. Along with that, he struggled with the perception that others had of him.

WE'RE NOT THAT DIFFERENT, BUT WE ARE DIFFERENT

I think that there's this romanticized notion that Hollywood has helped create, that there's two kinds of veterans. There's the broken PTSD veteran, and there's the absolute heroic superhero veteran. I don't think it's that easy to put us into one or the other of those categories. A lot of veterans are normal people who were willing to do extraordinary things. I consider myself normal. I think that what I experienced after leaving the army isn't all that much different, in some respects, from what other people go through in dealing with change—except for the war and combat part of it.

When I got out, I was a senior team leader. I plotted grid coordinates to help land a platoon of Rangers. We ran out of Black Hawk helicopters, and I was the first one to shoot and run at the enemy. I had these amazing teammates. I had this whole support system and ecosystem that I defined myself by. And the next day, that team, that purpose was gone. I was left without a vision of what I wanted to do, no sense of purpose. Everything that I had used to define myself was gone. I was around a bunch of college kids in Los Angeles who were drinking beers and chasing girls, and the hardest thing in their life was getting their homework done.

That's not to discredit them. We had lived two different versions of life. My past reality was different from theirs—drastically different. It got hard for me, because I didn't have that frame of reference anymore—the guys around me in the army who were experiencing the same things I was. Now I was living with and hanging out with a bunch of guys who didn't share the same experiences I had. I went down the rabbit hole that a lot of guys do—self-medicating, becoming resentful, almost taking on the victim role, *Woe is me. I blame the world for not understanding what I went through.*

It really took a year and a half and some good friends kicking me in the ass and saying, "Hey, idiot, right now you're the creator of your own calamity, so that means you can create your own reality. So are you going to soak in sorrow and be a miserable little shit, or are you going to go after it and define your destiny?"

I can see now that I really lost my way and had forgotten some of the things the military taught me. You can prepare for any situation, but the unknown is always going to happen. More likely than not, you're going to be presented with a situation that you weren't expecting. And there is no "I can't do this." When you're on a target and you're dealing with a hypercomplex situation, it's up to you to be a creative problem solver. And you can't say, "I can't do this." You have to do something. You might not make the right decision, but you have to make a decision.

Over time, I learned that I had control. I was going to school. I was doing some personal protection work. I wasn't loving either. I was hanging out with people who were almost always negative. One morning I got a call from a Ranger buddy who told me to get my shit together. I drove to my apartment; broke up with my girlfriend; called my dad, almost in tears, and said, "Dad? Can I come home?"

CHANGE IS HARD; CHANGE IS GOOD

I drove back to Santa Barbara and moved into a bedroom—you know, twenty-four years old in the back of my dad's kind of run-down house—and said, "Well, time to start my life over." And it was scary as hell, but it was the most refreshing feeling ever, because I said, "Every decision I make right now changes the course of my life for better or for worse, and I own that." And there was a sense of leadership and responsibility that was given to me that goes, *Every-*

thing forward at this point in my life is up to me to change, and I get to decide where it goes. And it's up to nobody else other than myself, kind of the same way as being team leader, where how I decide to assault the objective, how I decide to manage my team, how I decide to maneuver, is the course between me dying and my teammates dying or us living. And on a less consequential way, that's how it was in civilian life.

And that's really why I started going to college, started developing these skills, and then applied to become a contractor and get back overseas. Because I knew I kind of had to wean myself off of war because I missed it so much, that it was like I'd been smoking cigarettes in Ranger battalion and I wanted to quit, but I at least had to put that nicotine patch on. And that was kind of what, for me, contracting was. I still got to be around former Special Operations guys. I had a mission that was filled with purpose, but it wasn't as severe and dangerous, necessarily, as Ranger battalion. And I could focus on bettering myself, bettering my psychology, and creating skills that will, hopefully, make me into a better person and businessperson.

YOU HAVE TO START SOMEWHERE

One thing that successful businesspeople do is to recognize a critical need and fill it with a product. For me, that meant creating YouTube content that filled a void.

When I started making videos, there wasn't a lot of content out there that really showed the full scope of what Special Operations guys actually are like. I think that it was always the chiseled, barrel-chested guy giving that motivational speech. And granted, that's a great aspect of our community. But people forget that we joke in the team rooms every night before we're going out. Like, "Well, I hope if someone gets shot, it's Evans tonight because," dah dah dah dah. Obviously, we'd never want that to happen. But comedy in these tragic and dire situations brings a little relief and a little mental uplift to the team that actually makes you more effective.

I wanted to apply that perspective to entertainment so people could see yes, we're professionals, yes, we can go out and jump out of a Black Hawk in the middle of the night and hunt terrorists, but we can also laugh. And a lot of us have other talents. We can be creative and artistic and have these amazing attributes that we bring to the community and to the veteran experience.

I've tried over the years to make people laugh and team-build, build a community and show that it's okay to be a little irreverent and have a macabre sense of humor. I think that's how a lot of people manage their day-to-day lives in these really challenging workplaces as Special Operations, or even on a FOB in Iraq or Afghanistan, or law enforcement, or EMS people that are having to pick up bodies off the street every night. I think we all have that dark humor, and a lot of general society doesn't want to accept that that's how a lot of us deal with it. And I felt that we had to show them that, *Hey, guys, this is what we do sometimes because this is how we manage this crazy life that we signed up for.*

During the Ranger selection process, which was super intense, I'd make a fart sound or butt rub against another guy to get a laugh. Some of the other super-serious guys hated that, and the thing was, a lot of those super-serious guys didn't qualify. They quit because the pressure got to them. The jokes were a way of forgetting that we were cold, tired, and hungry.

In battalion we used to binge-watch *Family Guy*. I love slapstick humor, Will Ferrell. When I first started writing skits, I just drew from my experiences and other contractors' experiences. We'd sit around swapping stories and I had my notepad out. That's where a lot of the "You Might Be a Veteran If . . ." material came from.

A SERIOUS SIDE TO BEING FUNNY

When I moved back with my dad, I still had no purpose. I was drinking too much, getting into fights. I had all this energy but I was directing it the wrong ways. I wasn't making myself better. After I started making the videos, I realized something. They were a win for me. A small win, but everybody needs those. Those small wins build on one another, and the incremental success starts to put you on a positive path. It takes a lot of work stringing those wins together, and you have to learn from some of the failures that get mixed in there. I told myself I wanted to get on YouTube. I had to literally google "how to make a film." I had to buy a camera. I had some success. I bought a better camera. The videos became a little more sophisticated. I learned some things. Those incremental wins, and incremental training and education, will get you to the goal. I learned that in the military, forgot about it for a while, but figured it out again. But you've got to enjoy it along the way. Destinations normally aren't as good as you expect them to be. The travel to get there is usually the best memory.

I eventually transitioned from making funny videos to becoming a more serious entrepreneur, and now focus mainly on veterans' issues.

Generally speaking, veterans in this culture are respected. It's not like it was with Vietnam veterans. No one is spitting at us when we come home. That's a great thing. Conversely, there is a perception problem regarding our generation of warriors. A lot of people think that war breaks you. I think that a lot of people on the East and West Coasts believe, *Oh, they're an at-risk community because they went to war.* I completely disagree with that sentiment. I really want to change that narrative.

One of the reasons our company hires veterans is because they have such a diverse skill set. Also, veterans are good at not responding emotionally but focusing on the rational and carrying forward the mission by any means necessary. I wish that more employers, companies, and enterprises realized that. Veterans are amazing assets. You aren't giving a veteran a break by hiring one; you're giving yourself a break because you're bringing on board someone who is highly capable.

And veterans need to realize that about themselves. This is a two-way street. We need to do a better job of understanding that we do have workplace experience. We did have a career. We did have management and leadership experience. If you looked at my résumé, it's like more than four hundred direct action raids, former team leader, which might not translate to work experience. "Team leader" is synonymous with "manager," right? The military is an organization. You won't survive in it long if you don't figure out how it operates and your role in it.

I'm not that smart a guy. I just outwork my intelligence. I just grind away every single day. I try to be a sponge. I'm thirty-three years old. Black Rifle Coffee is continuing to grow right now. I'm the number two guy in the company. I'm not "qualified" for this. What I can do is hire people around me that are smarter than me and learn from them, so that on a daily basis I can make informed, educated decisions and learn from my mistakes. I think I'm doing well because unlike many in the social-media-driven world we live in, I don't focus on *Hey, look at me! I'm successful!* Just like in the military, people need to chill out and focus on showcasing their work rather than the image of success—the fancy watch, the car, or their own pretty self. Just my opinion on focusing on the tangibles which make a difference.

Business is hard for me. It's all about building relationships and, despite a lot of what I put out there, I'm an introvert. People who know me well get that. People who don't might be surprised to learn this about me. I call myself a gregarious introvert. I can turn it on when I have to. When I don't, I go back inside.

CONTINUING TO SERVE

One of the sayings that defines my life to this point is, "If not me, then who?" That's a variation on Isaiah, from the Bible, stepping up. One time I didn't want to step up to the plate was after Brehm and Barraza were killed. The powers that be were leading the after-action review. They asked who was with 1st Squad that made the initial entry. I was a lowly E-3 private. I didn't want to speak up. I looked around, and I was the only guy in the team room who wasn't wounded. I knew it was up to me. I was terrified. Just thirty seconds before that, I'd learned that those two men I admired so much had died. I stood there. I took a few deep breaths. I held back my tears. I looked at the first sergeant. I looked at the company commander. I said the first word, and then the next ones all fell in place after that. I kept it together.

That was the first time I think I really made an effort to avoid the victim mentality. There are always going to be times in your life when things aren't going to go the way you want them to. It's up to you how you react to the world and what it hands you. We have a saying, "Psychology is more contagious than the flu." You can put some positive things out in the world or some negative things. Both can be powerful.

I tell people sometimes that they should look at their phones and the most commonly used emojis. If they're mostly negative ones, then that says something about how they're interacting with the world and what they're putting out there. Success is all about fixing shit that's not working right, working through some complex problems, sometimes tragic ones. You have to slowly sort through the drama and all the shit that the world throws at us and come out on the other side stronger. We get lost sometimes in the frivolous drama and the false constructs that society creates. There's always someone or some force telling us how we should act, who we should be. We let other people influence us, put us in little boxes. We're all more than just what a checklist might say.

I've had times when I had to be violent. Now what I really hope for is that people will be kinder in life—to themselves and to other people. Especially here in the US. If you were born here, you won the lottery. You got the golden ticket to pursue opportunities and you have the individual freedom to pick which one to take on. I think more people need to realize that and not take it for granted. This is a very special place.

★ ★ ★

CHAPTER 7

LIEUTENANT COLONEL (RET.)
SCOTT MANN
UNITED STATES ARMY

It's nerve-racking, but at the end of the day when you see the effects, when you see the exponential power that comes from indigenous people handling their own affairs, you realize that one of the most effective things that a Green Beret can do for his country is to help put that kind of capacity in place.

Slipping onto a target in the dead of night always produces a pucker factor. Doing it with a battalion of completely untested Afghan National Army (ANA) soldiers—most of them illiterate teenagers—really had all of our guts churning. The helicopters dropped us off into seven different landing zones. From the time we hit the ground, we were in contact with the Taliban.

There were times when you could see the vapor trail of those ANA guys running away from the battle. Our Green Beret sergeants, who are, in my professional opinion, the finest operators on the planet, they would grab them by the stack and swivel and bring them back into the fight, however they needed to do it, and stand right there, shoulder to shoulder with them, and help them gather courage. Sometimes the Green Berets would be the only ones fighting while the rest turned and ran. It was hard. But all in all, the ANA performed pretty darn well.

★★★★★★★★★★★★★★★★★★★★★★★★★★★★★★★★★★★★★★

Scott spent twenty-three years serving in the United States Army. He was a member of the Special Operations community for fifteen of those years. He was proud to be a Green Beret. During his career, he was involved in a variety of tasks—foreign internal defense (helping train and advise another country's troops), counterinsurgency operations, stability missions, and combat missions across the globe. From deployments in Colombia, Ecuador, Peru, and Panama, he transitioned to the main sites of our global war on terror—Iraq and Afghanistan.

While there, he designed and implemented the army's Special Operations Village Stability program, along with the Afghan Police Program in Afghanistan, to help Afghans stand up against the Taliban on their own. From 2010 to 2011 he was responsible for creating and using the training methods that brought up to speed more than four thousand Special Operations personnel who ultimately served in Afghanistan. An exemplary leader of men, an accomplished communicator and strategic thinker, Scott served with distinction wherever he was assigned, whatever task he took on. He was especially proud to wear the green beret, the symbol of the historic Special Forces unit. The beret, as President John F. Kennedy said in 1962, was a "symbol of excellence, a badge of courage, a mark of distinction in the fight for freedom."

Today he lives in Riverview, Florida, with his wife, Monty, and their children, Cody, Cooper, and Brayden.

Appropriately, Scott continues to serve in a variety of capacities. He is an advisery board member for Spirit of America.

He also founded a charitable organization called The Heroes Journey. Its mission is to help warriors find their voice and tell their story of transition. As Scott points out, "Every year, two hundred thousand veterans transition from military service into civilian life. It's a challenging time that often results in loss of identity and changes so significant it seems like the veteran is changing planets. For our warriors to live the life of prosperity they deserve, they must rediscover their voice and tell their story."

The organization gets its name from literature professor Joseph Campbell's description of how in all cultures at all times, heroic stories followed a similar pattern (think of the early Star Wars films and Luke Skywalker). The first of those stages in the Hero's Journey is the Call to Action.

★★★★★★★★★★★★★★★★★★★★★★★★★★★★★★★★★★★★★★★

SCOTT'S CALL

I decided to become a Green Beret when I was fourteen. I grew up in a little logging town in Mount Ida, Arkansas. My dad was a forester, fought wildfires, so we always lived in these little logging towns. We didn't even have a stoplight. And a Green Beret walked into our soda shop one day—his name was Mark. He was home on leave in his full regalia, his dress uniform. And as soon as he walked in, man, that's what I wanted to do. I can still remember it. And I was a scrawny runt of a kid, and that dude, just looking at him, I knew that's what I wanted to be. And I didn't even know what he was. But he was a Special Forces officer, and he sat down with me there in the soda shop and explained to me what Green Berets were and what they did, and I just fell in love with the concept right away.

Encountering Mark wasn't my only inspiration—I remember hearing the Sergeant Barry Sadler song "The Ballad of the Green Berets" playing on the radio. The song had hit the top of the Billboard charts back in 1966, but still received airplay when I was a kid.

My dad also had a copy of January 1965's *National Geographic* magazine. On the cover was a photo of a Green Beret, another Special Forces captain. The story told of him working with the Montagnard people in Vietnam. They were about to overrun his camp. They'd done it to a few others. Instead of deciding to gun up against the Montagnards, the captain decided the better approach was to participate in a friendship ceremony with them. He found a tribal elder and put on loincloths, and that convinced the rest of them to take up arms with the American troops. And I just thought, *Holy cow, these guys are amazing!*

Also, my dad was a straight-up servant leader. He was from the mountains of North Carolina, so he had this easygoing Southern drawl to him. He was very, very intelligent—dialed in, really focused.

But he always put everyone at ease. He always made you feel like you were the most important person in the world. A great listener. All the other firefighters just loved him. I wanted to have that kind of effect on people. I wanted to be able to serve them in the same way my father did. My mom was a schoolteacher—taught me in fact—so I grew up in a family of civil servants. All of the teachers in that little town lifted us up and nurtured me in a way that prepared me for some tough situations that would come down the road. They gave me a real common-sense way of looking at the world in a small-town compassionate kind of way.

Because of the influences I had, my call to action had a lot to do with the unique mission of the Green Berets. What I tell people first of all is that Green Berets are very different than Navy SEALs. Navy SEALs typically go in as a surgical strike–type unit, which most Special Operations Forces are. They go in, they hit a target, and they're out quickly. They usually do the mission unilaterally.

Green Berets are different. They parachute in below the noise, and generally walk into trust-depleted, conflict-riddled areas and connect with the locals there. They build relationships, and then, over a long period of time, they help those locals stand up on their own. Our mission is to work by, with, and through indigenous peoples. Another way to think of it is that Green Berets are relationship-based connectors who happen to be lethal when necessary. They're able to go into places with a twelve-person team and ride out with twelve thousand, like the horse soldiers did right after 9/11.

CROSSING THE THRESHOLD—LEAVING HOME

After graduating from Mount Ida High School, where he was a part of the ROTC program and received a three-year scholarship, Scott attended and graduated from the University of Central Arkansas in Conway (the alma mater of NBA Hall of Famer Scottie Pippen). Because he'd seen his father working as the incident commander with US Forest Service, Scott dreamed of becoming a detachment commander in the army. He began his career in the Quartermaster Corps (one of the army's logistics branches whose primary function is supply) before successfully fulfilling his Green Berets aspirations. Scott is a graduate of "Pineland University"—a reference to having participated in Robin Sage, the world's largest military role-playing exercise. Generations of civilian North Carolinians have participated as role players. It was there that he first gained insight into how the Green Berets truly operated.

I got an appreciation for those innate, old-school interpersonal skills that are so uniquely relevant to the kind of work that we do. I think that sometimes the movies do a disservice by leading us to believe that everything is direct action, and there's some truth to that. But the larger reality is that what moves people in these trust-depleted areas are the human connections that you make, and that's our bread and butter.

If you go back to the origins of Special Forces out of the OSS (Office of Strategic Services) in World War II, that organization dropped small Jedburgh teams into occupied Europe to mobilize partisans to fight back against the Nazis. Once World War II ended, that organization split into two groups—the Central Intelligence Agency and the 10th Special Forces Group.

TESTS, ALLIES, AND ENEMIES

I believe that post-9/11, the Green Berets temporarily lost their way. In our exuberance to exact payback on the Taliban and al-Qaeda in Afghanistan—and I was, unfortunately, part of this evolution—we moved away from some phases of our mission. We started to place an emphasis on surgical targeting and took more of a direct action approach. The "by, with, and through" thing got out of balance. We were out in these rural areas, but our ultimate metric was how many Taliban we were knocking down a day, and it was not capacity-building of the Afghan National Army or doing any of the other things that we typically did to help indigenous people help themselves. It was about man-hunting.

It took me a while, but in time, I recognized the importance of taking on all phases of the Special Forces mission.

When I got into Special Forces, the first ten years of my career were working down in Colombia and the Andean Ridge area, primarily combat advising Colombian forces against the FARC. And there were episodic moments of conflicts. My first exposure to true open combat was Afghanistan 2004–2005 on my first rotation in country. I was the mission commander for a battalion operating in southern Afghanistan. We really wanted to try to get the Afghan National Army up on its feet. Only thing was, there wasn't one. After the Soviets left, the country fell into civil war and there was no ANA to speak of.

Still, we were champing at the bit to use our experience in foreign internal defense. A major in 7th Special Forces Group, I was selected to be the mission commander for, really, the first-ever battalion-level maneuver mission against the Taliban. Operation Nam Dong took place in Oruzgan Province. It was named after a firebase in Vietnam where a Special Forces team had earned the Congressional Medal of

Honor, led by Captain Roger Donlon. And one of the primary teams that was going to participate in this Afghan mission had the same detachment number, 726. And it also happened to be my old detachment number from when I was a captain, so it was kind of ironic.

The mission set was heavily saturated with Taliban senior leadership. An infantry battalion, the only true US presence, was placed up there in a Fort Apache kind of construct deep in this Taliban sanctuary. The battalion was going to be pulled out of that area, and they were not going to be backfilled. We were approaching the summer fighting season, and we knew that if that happened and there was no disruption at all in that province, there was going to be hell to pay. So I nominated to the two-star headquarters and Bagram a way that we could actually backfill the infantry battalion with a large force of Afghan National Army combat advised by Special Forces, because that was the only choice we had.

At the time, though, understand that there were no ANA soldiers operating as a maneuver force at all, not even at the platoon level. None of these soldiers had ever seen combat collectively. So when I went up to pitch this mission, it was pretty audacious. I was basically saying that we would infiltrate under cover of darkness with a large contingent of ANA and a handful of Green Beret advisers. And then when the infantry flew out, we would fly in and basically move to contact and duke it out with the Taliban. Then we would reset on the same base where the infantry had been and put our flag in the ground.

And the two-star command approved it. They asked us what we would need to get it done. I had a little laundry list of what I needed. We asked for three Chinook helicopters, a couple of Black Hawks, and two 105 mm howitzers to be brought in with my headquarters. We asked for a dedicated medevac and even a drone to be committed to us. Now remember, this is '04. At this point in the war, it was unheard of for Special Forces to do this kind of maneuver. That really hadn't happened since '01, when 5th Group went in with the Northern Alliance. We had some more time to prepare, but most of these soldiers were around fourteen years of age. They were illiterate. The Afghan National Army soldier is not like the American soldier. There's a point of pride for anyone to be in the US military as a volunteer. You're representing your family, your community.

Afghanistan is a tribal society. Most of those who joined the military did so out of desperation. They came from the city because they'd been ousted, for whatever reason, from their tribal community. We had huge desertion rates. But we kept at it and kept it.

In April 2005, those untested Afghan kids and a small group of Green Berets arrived at Fire Base Cobra in the deep darkness of an Afghan night. The pucker factor was high.

From the time we hit the ground, including my headquarters element, we were in contact. It was about a ten-day sustained engagement with the Taliban. They tried to mass on us multiple times because they felt like the ANA, they'd never seen them before. They had to be untested. But we were able to use artillery fire and close air support to really just hammer them. We pushed them back. And behind that, we brought in multiple civil affairs teams. We brought in med caps. We even brought in what we called mobile mullahs from Kandahar, moderate Islamic mullahs who went out and conducted *shura*s (Islamic style consultations or meetings) with locals. All of this was a part of what we called "capacity building"—getting the locals in a position to defend and take care of themselves.

When the dust cleared, we lost one Green Beret, we had several wounded, and several Afghan National Army had been killed. We established a permanent base for the ANA at Tarin Kowt, which is just right down the road from where we were conducting the operation. Those units are still there to this day. It was how we established the provincial flag in the ground for the Afghan National Army in that area.

I think people don't understand, with Special Forces work, that the easiest thing in the world is just to gun up and do it yourselves. Have the Afghans pull left and right flank security, and you go hit the target. That meets the minimum token requirement for including Afghans in the fight. But we didn't do that. We put them at the forefront, and we insisted on them using their systems, their comms, their logistics, and we were right there with them. And then only when it started to falter or fail would we replace it with our own. And then we would correct it and have them do it again. It's nerve-racking, it's scary as shit, but it's the only way to truly build capacity in a nation like that.

THE ORDEAL

Scott understands that the media and the American public often didn't find the kinds of success stories he experienced to be as sexy as combat operations. The fatigue from a long conflict was real, the news cycle was constantly churning, and stories like the Green Berets resolving a factional division of two local tribes over a water issue wouldn't make for glowing headlines or webpage clicks. The reality was, by helping the Afghans resolve that water conflict themselves, which the Taliban would have exploited to its benefit, they aimed to take a chunk out of the Taliban's power over those people.

American intel revealed that Osama bin Laden himself had taken note of the Green Berets' effectiveness. He understood that their working with tribal elders was one of the biggest threats he faced. That was especially true since 2009, when Special Forces went from supporting six villages to 113 in the span of eighteen months.

Scott believes that is the untold story of his war.

What we recognized ten years in was that our ideal scenario of projecting democracy and a uniform Afghan National Army just didn't resonate with Pashtun tribes. What did resonate with them was a local security force that was village-based, a very loose relationship with their government, and elders who were empowered to resolve disputes at their level. Once we started doing that and helping them get back what the Taliban had taken, we saw a real brushfire movement of Afghans standing up for themselves.

Until we moved out of those firebases and into the local communities, we didn't realize how decimated those local village structures had been by forty years of war. Most of the elders, who had been intimidated by a succession of bad guys like the Soviets, warlords, and then the Taliban, hadn't even gone back to their villages. Those societies were broken. Those villagers didn't care about national elections. They wanted to be able to grow their crops uninterrupted. They wanted to be able to resolve their own problems. We would help them build their capacity to do those things, and if we weren't able to do that effectively, we'd call in experts from the State Department and development experts like USAID.

To be fully successful at capacity building was going to take decades. We started too late. It was working well, but at a policy level, the appetite was just not there. We ended up bailing. It was nerve-racking work, but at the end of the day when you see the effects of it, when you see the exponential power that comes from indigenous people handling their own affairs, you realize that is one of the most effective things that a Green Beret can do for his country. When you put that kind of capacity in place, because it's an economy of force, it's a huge return on a minimal investment. It can be lasting and it can be enduring.

THE REWARD

In one of Scott's TED Talks, "Surrounded on Purpose," he addresses the issue of why someone would volunteer to take part in what can, on the surface, seem to be such a thankless task.

"For us, there really is something about our motto, *De Oppresso Liber*."

The Special Forces motto, loosely translated from Latin, means "to liberate the oppressed." More literally it means "from an oppressed man to a free one."

In a way, that is what Scott has been working toward in his post-military career, primarily through his Heroes Journey foundation. While "oppressed" may be too strong a word, many veterans have a difficult time making the transition from military life to civilian life. Scott experienced these struggles firsthand.

When I got home, the first year or so, I did contract work, and man, I tried to do what everybody told me to do. Get a job, a high-paying job, as a contractor. That was when the PTSD, the survivors' guilt, really came home in a terrible way, and I almost took my own life. When I came out on the other side of it, that's when I really fell in love with storytelling. It helped me come back into the sunlight. I started teaching from the stage and using the Green Beret interpersonal skills.

Most people, years and years into these things, still don't have much of a clue about what Green Berets in particular were doing in Afghanistan, Syria, and other places around the world. Our Special Forces soldiers have had more killed in action post-9/11 than all of the other Special Operations components combined. And it's because they operate in these squishy environments where you don't hear a lot about what we still do and how we still are dying.

COMING HOME

The final stage of the Hero's Journey is coming home after being changed by battlefield experiences. Scott has dedicated much of his time since retiring from the army to assisting veterans with that transition.

I didn't realize how purpose-driven I was when I was in Special Forces, because it was all I knew. It's all I had ever wanted to do. So every day that my boots hit the floor, even on really crappy days, I was doing what I was born to do. And then when I took the uniform off and I walked away from it, I just thought, *Well, that part of my life is over*.

I didn't take the time to reorient my purpose. I didn't look at any of that. I just stepped into what I thought other people thought I should do, and it was a disaster. It was an unmitigated disaster. When you take the meaning out of a human's life, we die. And we just cannot operate without purpose. And I worry about that today. I see so many warriors coming home, and our family members, that are just disconnected from their purpose. And they're disconnected from their own personal narrative, which is just as bad.

My transition was so bad that when I came out of it on the other side, forming Rooftop Leadership and helping veterans by helping them tell their stories really helped me. Bringing forward the lessons of interpersonal human connection, for leaders here at home, gave me a renewed purpose. Otherwise, I don't know that I would have made it. Helping others truly helped me.

Another way that Scott has worked to share his story and to heal was by writing a play, *Last Out: Elegy of a Green Beret*. The main character, Danny Patton, is a composite character based on three team sergeants that Scott had. Danny Patton, killed early in the play, wants to go to Valhalla to rest and find peace. His deceased brothers return from there, and with their help, Danny relives important moments from his life. He discovers the troubling things that he has held on to and then lets go. Only then can he find the peace and rest of Valhalla. For Scott, writing and performing the play was as nerve-racking an experience as nearly anything he'd been through to that point. Just as in his military career, several mentors played a key role in helping him get the play produced. It's been featured on Tom Brokaw's *NBC Nightly News*, Fox News, and Fox Nation and will resume live performances in 2021.

But I tell you what, man. Every time I get ready to walk on that stage, I feel like I'm going on a mission. It is terrifying because it's so emotional. And it's everything from holding your buddy in his last moments to getting the phone call from the Afghan elder that the Taliban are in his house and you're no longer in the village. It's all that, and it's raw. It's super, super visceral. But it's been a great way, at least for me, to help people understand the impact of modern war. It is a Green Beret story, but there are a lot of universal singulars in it that I think have really promoted a lot of healing and understanding at a community level. And I think it's an example of how we can use storytelling to come home and heal. Sometimes that means telling your own story; sometimes it means sitting back and listening to others as they share theirs. We need to talk, but we also need to listen to one another, too.

You hear about people putting limits on free speech because someone else's speech is harmful to me. How is it possible then to have a civil discussion that keeps us free?

—*Sergeant Mat Best*

★

We're forever indebted to our military. Some of us believe that and some of us don't. Frankly, shame on the people that don't. But we live in America because we have people out there doing it and who will stand up and who will take the path less chosen and who will continue to sacrifice for everyone else's freedom.

—*Lieutenant Commander Caroline Johnson*

★

All the American public hears is "Endless wars!" and that's a meaningless statement. We're in South Korea still. Is that an endless war? We're still in Japan. Is that an endless war? Germany?

—*Lieutenant Commander Dan Crenshaw*

★

Warriors are willing to do something bigger than themselves even when the odds are stacked against them.

—*Staff Sergeant Jeremiah Workman*

PART III

CONTINUING TO SERVE

How do we have the patriotism of September 12 without the tragedy of September 11? That's what this country needs to go back to.

—*Sergeant Mat Best*

★

Being of service is the bedrock of being a warrior, because you put others before yourself. That leads to the tremendous camaraderie with your people in the field in combat, and that leads to the feeling of love and brotherhood. Love and brotherhood elevate elite units in the military to accomplish amazing things.

—*Captain Sean Parnell*

CHAPTER 8

LIEUTENANT COMMANDER (RET.)
DANIEL CRENSHAW
UNITED STATES NAVY

The ability to deal with adversity,
to accept pain, to be calm
under pressure—these are the
traits we look for. Some can
be taught, much is innate.

Everybody approaches a career in politics differently. Some just want to be a statesman. They don't really want to pick fights. They just want to work on a couple of pieces of legislation. They'll do some town halls, and they'll be very nonconfrontational. They're very afraid of creating waves. They're very careful about how they speak.

That's old politics.

That's not successful anymore.

The people are sick of it; they don't trust it.

That's not to say some people don't like it, and that's not to say that it's not successful in some places.

But that's never who I was. I pick more fights than almost all politicians. There's not that many in my category that engage in so many battles—political battles. The president clearly engages in the most. It's obvious. He picks fights everywhere; he doesn't discriminate. I'm much more cautious than he is, or much more strategic in what battles I want to pick. But I do engage in them on a cultural level, a political level, and a policy level. And that's always what I wanted to do. I didn't get into it just to be quiet and have a long career. Well, I want a long career, but I think the key to a long career is making an impact, and there's a lot of ways to make an impact. And I think influence and communication are a huge part of that impact.

★★★★★★★★★★★★★★★★★★★★★★★★★★★★★★★★★★★★★★

Congressman Dan Crenshaw has certainly made an impact since being elected to the House of Representatives in 2019 for Texas's Second Congressional District. He ran as a Republican in the primary with very little previous legislative experience and virtually no money to take on candidates with deeper pockets and more political and legislative experience. He won, like he has so often in life. Since taking office, he has gained in prominence within the Republican Party and is considered to be one of its young rising stars. That should come as no surprise given Congressman Crenshaw's bona fides.

When he was twelve, Congressman Crenshaw's father suggested he read Dick Marcinko's *Rogue Warrior*. Marcinko was a Navy SEAL and the man who first commanded SEAL Team 6. His memoir fired the imaginations of many future SEAL team members. Congressman Crenshaw possessed a keen sense of adventure at an early age (he originally thought he wanted to be a spy), but after reading that book, he told himself that a SEAL was who he wanted to become. In Congressman Crenshaw's mind, there is an important distinction between deciding what you want to do with your life and deciding what kind of person you want to be. Many of the decisions he's made in life have been based around the latter.

His father worked in the petroleum industry, and the family traveled a great deal: Scotland, Egypt, Ecuador, and Colombia. As a result, Congressman Crenshaw developed a perspective on the world that deepened his appreciation for America and what it offered.

He also wanted to model himself after his mother. For five years, Susan Carol Crenshaw fought a battle against breast cancer. Her positivity and refusal to give in to a victim's mentality had a profound effect on him long after she passed away when he was ten.

A 2006 graduate of Tufts University with a degree in international relations, Congressman Crenshaw was also enrolled in the naval ROTC program there. He commissioned in the navy immediately after graduation. He served for ten years, experienced five tours of duty, and was medically retired in 2016. In 2012, while on an operation in Helmand Province, Afghanistan, an IED explosion seriously wounded him. He lost his right eye and very nearly lost the vision in his left. His recovery was miraculous, and he later deployed to Bahrain and South Korea.

He served with great distinction during his military career and was awarded two Bronze Stars, one with Valor; the Purple Heart; and the Navy and Marine Corps Commendation Medal with Valor, among many others.

★★

GETTING ON WITH THINGS

On June 15, 2012, while working in Afghanistan with my SEAL Team 3 teammates, our interpreter was just ahead of me. When he stepped on an IED, the force of the blast took off all his limbs. I felt like I'd been hit by a truck.

We all knew getting blown up by an IED would suck. Losing an eye is tough. Losing two eyes would have been tougher. I made the decision to have risky surgery to save my one remaining eye, knowing that if it failed, I'd lose my vision entirely. The choice was easy. Of course you take the risk. I was going to lose my vision eventually if I didn't opt for the procedure. What did I have to lose that wasn't going to be lost to me later?

I also knew this. As bad as I had it, lots of people have had it worse than me. Lots of others had made the ultimate sacrifice. I've got the initials of eight of those guys tattooed on my chest. So even when you're lying bleeding on the ground, unable to see much of anything, and later totally blind facedown in a bed for six weeks, you know what? Your buddies don't even get to have that chance because they're dead. That sounds morbid, but it's true. It should toughen your spine a little bit and make you feel grateful for being here at all. Too many people don't show gratitude for the new mission that they might have. They complain. They complain about the Veterans Administration. They complain about their disability payments. They complain about their lack of opportunity. Well, your buddies don't get to complain at all, and I think they would be grateful for anything.

Living with duty means having a duty to those who aren't able to complete their mission because they would want you to keep going. They would want you to live with a purpose. That's a message for civilians; that's a message for veterans.

I say this with 100 percent confidence: Each of those eight guys was among the best of us. When we got up and spoke at their funerals, we weren't lying when we said that this guy was one of the best SEALs we ever knew. They were the greatest public servants we ever knew, and that story needs to be told. We're not sending miscreants overseas; we're not sending victims; we're sending leaders. The guys I served with on the teams were some of the smartest, brightest, funniest, most capable people in the world.

And these guys weren't victims. These are guys who would do it again and again and again. They might take a step in a different direction so they don't take that bullet or take that explosion. They might get on a different helicopter, but they would do it again.

There's a notion out there that service members are victims somehow, that they were being used by some government overlord to do their political bidding. That's not true. We're an all-volunteer force and we love what we do. We understand that there are bad people out there that seek to do harm against the United States' interests. We are willing to go out there and fight them.

LIVING THE LIFE YOU CHOSE

Everybody I knew who became a SEAL wanted to be one for a long time. You wanted this. You knew that you were, or wanted to be, an outside-the-box thinker, a sort of renegade or rebel, but also a strictly disciplined soldier. So you became that before you got to BUD/S (basic underwater demolition/SEAL training). BUD/S just made you prove it and then trained you how to harness that. You learn how to exist in two different mental states: those of an ultra-aggressive combatant and a chivalrous gentleman. And you can instantaneously transition between the two. That's a warrior.

Self-imposed suffering, especially with others, builds true mental toughness. Anytime you push yourself past your previously perceived limits, you become a stronger person, psychologically and physically. BUD/S isn't the only thing that does that. It's multiple deployments, being away from home and family and friends. It's thinking through the possibility of pain and suffering and becoming at peace with them. People break down mentally because some weakness surprises them. They'd never thought about it before because they haven't toughened themselves.

In BUD/S the failures are more surprising than the successes. A lot of times, the most athletic, the fittest, the physically strongest candidates were the ones who quit. They should have been able to just crush it, but they didn't. Part of that is because they spent too much time on physical preparation and not enough on mental preparation. They believed that because of their physicality, their athleticism, they wouldn't be so surprised when faced with immediate failure. Those failures happen fast in BUD/S. Your body fails constantly. That's what the program is designed to do to you. It is not physically possible to do everything that is being demanded of you. So you break down; you can't do every repetition of every exercise.

We called them beatdowns for a reason. The instructors want us to break down and run away with our tail between our legs. They keep pressing us to go on, even after you thought that the activity was over. That happens to you over and over again. Your muscles fail you. And the instructors understand that difference between quitting—a failure of the will—and failing—your body giving out when you have already pushed yourself past what you once perceived as your limit. They respect the fact that you hung in there long enough to truly fail.

That's probably why you see so much anxiety and increasing suicide in our larger society. We have the most comfortable society the world has ever known. And that's good; I'm glad we do. But it's also made some people weak, and they break down when confronted with suffering.

If you want to be a person who doesn't freak out just because you're scared or whatever else you're facing, then decide to be that person. Every time you fall short of that goal, look back on that situation and tell yourself you're going to do better next time. Eventually you will.

FEAR AND LIVING

For us, fear was a healthy response in some situations. You have to compartmentalize it, and you have to use it because it was often what kept us alive. One of the biggest problems I had in working with Afghans and Iraqis was that they don't fear the same way we do. They don't appear to value their own lives the way that we do.

In the US military, we have our own EOD (explosive ordnance disposal) specialists. They would be sent out first to scan for IEDs and other explosives. They were very precise and careful. Later, when we would send out Iraqi or Afghani EOD specialists, since this was their country they were defending, after all, they would walk around waving the metal detector. They were just going through the motions, not understanding, or not caring, about the consequences. They just didn't care. And I've watched them do this right after one of their buddies just got blasted, his legs blown off. They'd continue to walk carelessly. I was saying to myself, *Are you guys out of your minds?*

Fear should be a driver for self-preservation, but you cannot let it drive your emotional state either. This is the delicate balance that SEALs must walk: between stoicism and rational respect for danger.

Thanks to his surgeons, the support of his family and friends, and in particular his now wife, Tara, Dan was able to recover from his eye injuries and resumed active duty. With the help of a special contact lens or glasses, the vision in his remaining eye is correctable to nearly 20/20. Eventually, in 2016, despite his strenuous objections, he was medically retired from the navy. Always interested in government and policy, he earned a master's degree from Harvard University's John F. Kennedy School of Government in 2017. His views on government and policy were also shaped by his experience living, and going to school, overseas.

A VIEW FROM AFAR

It took me a while to really appreciate what we have here in the US. I was very accustomed to seeing, and was therefore a bit desensitized to, extreme poverty—especially as I traveled and lived in Egypt and South America. Attending high school in Colombia, the only American at the school, I was very aware of the political situation there. You couldn't help but be. It was a dangerous place. The risk of getting kidnapped was high. Our car was shot at once. The president of Colombia's son attended the same school, so there was an armed presence on campus guarding him. A civil war was underway, so we all knew the basics of the situation.

I developed a greater sense of patriotism as a result of being there. America was always a punching bag for everybody in the world, just because it was the biggest show in town. I witnessed a lot of shallow foreign policy thinking on the part of classmates and adults. I found myself having to defend my country a lot, but I was always successful in doing so.

I always knew that the "ugly American" existed, and I was never that. I learned Spanish. I did the things Colombians did. I engaged in the culture because I think that's how things should be. Just like I think that immigrants to this country should do the same thing. Those experiences gave me some perspective on the multicultural ideal that you see on the left, where all cultures are good and we should just love and accept the diversity. According to those on the left, then, if an American city turns into a non-American city, that should be celebrated. Well, I don't believe that; there is no other country that believes that. Colombians expected me to learn Spanish. They were proud of their culture and I was proud to be a part of their culture. Those experiences certainly inform my political reasoning to a degree.

POLICY AND POLITICS

I'm not sure what drew me to politics. The latter part of my military career, I became a bit more political, not going any further than reading about politics and policy—much more of the latter than the former. Mostly, I was always interested in making a persuasive argument. That's why I'm a conservative. I want to look at data points and reasoned positions. I think I was always wired as a conservative. I became more active politically because I was just so sick of seeing the wrong arguments being endlessly promoted without any real solid pushback. This stems back to my SEAL problem-solving skill set, so I love framing the argument. I love debating. There's a kind of positive debate that goes on in the teams. If you have a mission, what's the best way to accomplish it? Everybody agrees on a goal, but not how to achieve it. And the reasoning isn't based on "I feel like this would be better." No, it's "I think this approach will be more effective because . . ."

Then, the best approach, the best tactics, got implemented. We didn't engage in philosophical debate. It was all very pragmatic and problem centered—tactical. Another way to look at it was that we were engaged in a policy debate. What are we going to do?

I was always interested in policy and figuring out what's the best approach to governing. That moved me beyond the single-issue, direct action kind of thing we did within the teams. It became, for me, about more than one action or objective. If you care about the way you govern, then you care about many different policies. If you want to have a broad effect on governance and policies, then you have to enter into politics. If you want to focus on one policy, you can do that without entering into politics.

Politics is the social manifestation of a set of policies. When I speak to kids, I let them know that there's a crucial difference between politics and policy. If you want to go into politics, then you have to be a representative of other people. To do that, you have to be able to communicate well. So before you decide to run for office, you have to ask yourself a few questions: Do you care about just one policy or issue? Are you good at communicating? Are you able to frame and win an argument? What are you good at?

I don't think that all elected officials or candidates think through answers to these, and lots of candidates don't win because they quit on that notion of self-examination.

For me, politics happened overnight when an opportunity presented itself. Because the military makes you think you have to be uber-prepared for everything, I thought that maybe I'd run for a seat in about ten years.

In 2018, Crenshaw ran for Congress. He had worked briefly as a military legislative assistant for Congressman Pete Sessions (R-TX). When Hurricane Harvey hit the Houston area, Dan returned to Texas and volunteered in the relief efforts. Inspired by the determination and resilience he saw, and at the urging of national security analyst John Noonan, he announced his candidacy for the Second Congressional seat in November 2017. He was well ahead of his projected ten-year preparation schedule, but well behind in terms of creating a team to support his run.

THINKING TACTICALLY

We did it in three months. I had to file papers in December and the primary election was on March 3. The only good thing was that all of the candidates were working under that same time pressure because Congressman Ted Poe announced his retirement so suddenly. Otherwise, none of the nine of us who ran in the primary would have bothered. You just didn't stand a chance against an incumbent.

One of my opponents was a woman named Kathaleen Wall. She spent $6.5 million in those three months. That's a lot of money in any race, but that's a hell of a lot of money in that short a time period. So everybody in the district was receiving her mailers. She was advertising during the Super Bowl, during the Olympics. I remember thinking, *Jeez, there's no way I can beat that name recognition.*

So I just simplified my problem solving and mission statement, just like you would in any kind of military operation. I need as many people as possible to know my name and to kind of like me. That's what running for office is. Know who you are and like you. It's really that simple.

So how do you get them to know your name? Get their attention. Advertise. How do you pay for that? Fund-raise. I didn't have a whole lot of time, so that didn't go particularly well. I didn't even get a viable campaign team together until February. These people were strangers to me, but I had to put some trust in them. We continued to attack this like it was military operation. Strategic position of signage became a priority. I didn't know a whole lot about marketing, but I'm not stupid, either, and I knew what would catch people's attention—a picture of a guy wearing an eye patch.

In Texas, you are allowed to do early mail-in voting. A lot of older residents take advantage of that. Well, by early February when some of those ballots were going in, we hadn't even done a mailer. Of course, we didn't get those votes.

One of my other main competitors was a state representative named Kevin Roberts. He had already been elected to office, obviously, so he had an infrastructure already in place. He comes from a very wealthy family, so had that monetary advantage as well. All nine candidates were conservative Republicans, so it was going to be hard to differentiate yourself from the others who were running. I came up with the line "I'm going to be more than a vote. I'm going to be a lion for your cause."

It truly was an uphill battle; I had to work really hard. I knew my strengths, and fortunately in primaries you have a low turnout, so I was able to impress where I really needed to impress. In our district all of the conservative clubs and Republican Women's clubs put on forums. These are activist voters, and they're concerned about issues and policies. I performed really well at these functions and at the debate.

On election day, early voting and mail-in ballots had been counted by 7 p.m. I was in third place with 20 percent of the vote. Kathaleen Wall was in second with 27 percent and Kevin Roberts was out in front with 33 percent. I was behind, way behind. I felt certain, though, that I'd won the election day voting. But did I win it by enough? That's tough. Lo and behold, by 3 a.m. when all the precincts were in, I ended up in second place by 155 votes.

I won the runoff election with 70 percent of the votes. The general election in November 2018 was closer, winning by only seven points. Both those victories rank pretty high in my personal achievements list. I did it with a lot of help, just like I was able to recover from my injuries and do a lot of other things because I had so much support. Tara has been a huge part of all of this.

WINNING IS NOT ENOUGH

I'm also proud of what we've done since the election. I've managed to build a brand that I'm proud of. Obviously, I also make a lot of people mad. I'm not a politician without conflict.

Running the first time, the flooding as a result of Harvey was a huge issue within the district. I'm pleased with the improvements we've made to mitigate future danger.

On the national policy front, I want to be persuasive, but I also want to get legislation done. You can do both. Some politicians think you can only do legislation, but in order to get your legislation through, you have to be able to communicate it effectively. I'm proud of my ability to do that. I also learn something new all the time. I have to be humble and acknowledge knowing what I don't know. I feel like I'm pretty good at that and not picking fights that I'm not going to win. That's a key judgment issue. On specific issues, I'm proud to have been a very prominent voice on immigration and the border.

My support of the strike against Iranian general Qasem Soleimani put me in a position I don't like. The left said, "Oh, you're just a defender of Trump."

No, I'm a defender of good decisions. I just want you to stop lying about the decision, that's all. And I'm proud of my role in that. It didn't necessarily result in any specific policy, but informing public opinion is just as important. And now I'm just proud to be a leading voice for a smart reopening of the economy and battling back these false binary choices between deaths and leaving people locked down and watching their livelihoods dissipate.

I'm proud of being able to think through complex issues and get to the facts and get to coherent solutions and to then be able to deliver a coherent message about that solution.

AN INFORMED CITIZENRY

I encourage the American public to look beyond the headlines. If you read beyond the headlines, not only will you be outraged, you'll be a better thinker. Even good journalists are defeated by bad headlines. They don't write the headlines. Editors do, and they are created more as clickbait than truth. They are designed to appeal on an emotional level. I can't make the media do anything different. I can't force them. I can shame them all day long, which is what I do, but they don't care. So many journalists are so left-wing that they are fighting an ideological battle. They'll do whatever it takes to drive their side's biases home. And that's sad for the good journalists who are out there writing good and fair pieces.

It's up to us as consumers of information to be smarter, to take control. The only way a problem gets fixed is if you fix it as an individual. Don't just read to confirm your own preconceived bias. Do your research. Wait to form an opinion. You do no harm when you say you don't know and you don't have an opinion. There's no shame in that. There's a lot of shame in having a strong opinion with no facts.

Too many people are very quick to feel a truth. You can't feel a truth. You can have feelings, but don't pretend that your feelings are what matter the most. Don't let your feelings drive your reality.

A lot of people, veterans and civilians, fall victim to victimhood. They feel like they are victims. What are you doing, then? You're removing power from yourself. Now you're letting somebody else have control over you. That's a terrible existence. Even if you were really unfairly treated, you have to tell yourself a story of overcoming that. It's the only way out. Period. Full stop.

CHAPTER 9

LIEUTENANT COLONEL
ADAM KINZINGER
UNITED STATES AIR FORCE

September 11, 2001, was
the moment when I said to
myself that there were far
more important things in
life for me to be doing than
selling computer stuff.

Using a classified asset, we were able to spot the van. When we informed the army's Delta unit of successful contact, I could hear the excitement in their radio operator's response. Not even the usual distortion the comms systems produced could hide the fact that this was one of the high-value targets we always hoped to help them get on to. I was glad that I wasn't the only one who was amped.

Flying in Iraq in support of Task Force 16 and Task Force 17 wasn't always everything I'd hoped it would be. A lot of days were just drilling holes in the sky between 5,000 and 8,000 feet. I knew that we weren't doing boots-on-the-ground operations, that I'd never know what it would be like to be down there getting shot at, but we were at least contributing intel for these capture/kill missions.

We followed the van for a few kilometers. For a couple of minutes it stopped, rendezvousing with another vehicle. The truck it met up with stayed put; the van drove off. We stayed with it for a while, losing contact with the vehicle when it came to a house and we had flown on the far side of the structure. After I turned the RC-26 to circle back, the van was in motion again. At that point, I wondered if maybe they had stopped and switched drivers, or whatever. By that time, the Delta unit was on target as well, using the coordinates my camera operator had relayed.

From above, we watched as they assaulted on that van. The flash of a large explosion was followed by a plume of smoke spiraling. Bad guys taken care of.

A few minutes later, the operators' control officer asked us if we still had eyes on the truck we'd reported seeing earlier. I swiveled my head and couldn't believe it. "Holy crap! I see it."

I talked my camera operator onto that location. He was able to get coordinates on it and relay them to the Delta guys. Our work done for the day, we returned to base.

Later, I was gratified to hear that more than a dozen heavily armed al-Qaeda fighters were killed. Command realized that this was a hot spot of terrorist activity. The Iraqi Army was rolled into the area.

★★

Congressman Adam Kinzinger (R-IL) still enjoys flying privately but especially to fulfill his duties as a member of the Air National Guard. Along with having a childhood fascination with war, he developed an early interest in politics. At the age of five, he was attending church services at the First Baptist Church. On the way home from services, he spotted a neon pink sign in someone's yard. As Adam tells it, "I asked my parents about that sign. It had John Lewis's name on it. He was an old-school Southern Democrat. My parents told me that he went to our church and was running for mayor. I just became obsessed with the idea of running for office and politics in general. I even made my own sign, at five years old, and I paraded up and down the street with it. We lived on a cul-de-sac, so not many cars came by and only a few people saw me. That didn't matter, the fire was lit."

Adam's political ambitions first blossomed—he was copresident of his seventh-grade student body—and then waned. "I went through a rebellious period. Everybody fights for their identity during that period. I realized it wasn't cool to be interested in the things I was. So in high school, I started to get into drinking and intentionally didn't get good grades, because getting good grades was uncool as well."

One thing that Adam did think was cool was warfare. He was a huge fan of the movie *Red Dawn*, and would have liked to have been among those teenagers defending the US from Russians taking over a small Colorado town. That seemed in keeping with his childhood fascination with the military. "I don't know where it comes from as a kid. I don't know if it comes from a heart of service. God kind of authors things into every person, and for me it was the military—the cool stuff, the weapons, the uniforms, aviation." He was also a huge fan of *Top Gun* but has stated that he lacked confidence in himself to believe that he could ever become a pilot.

At seventeen, Adam joined the Army Reserve, but he chose not to enlist. His focus shifted from being an infantryman to a marine, and he also thought of the National Guard and flying helicopters. He enrolled at Illinois State University but was dismissed for poor grades. He later reenrolled and never received a grade below an A.

After he graduated, his career vision sharpened on a point— he signed up with the air force with an active duty spot as a pilot. He wasn't keen on moving around a lot, and when a slot in the Air Guard became available, he took it.

As a twenty-year-old, he also ran for public office for the first time. He won a seat on the McLean County board and served from 1998 to 2003. In November 2003, he was commissioned as a second lieutenant and later earned his pilot wings. He has served in the Air Force Special Operations, Air Combat Command, Air Mobility Command, and Air National Guard. He had clearly developed the confidence necessary to purse that dream of piloting. After completing his wartime service, he ran for Congress and is now in his fifth term. He was recently selected by House minority leader Kevin McCarthy (R-CA) to serve on the China Task Force, which was empaneled to explore ways to investigate China's Communist Party. He was recently married and splits his time between his home in Channahon, Illinois, and the Washington, DC, area.

★★

UNDERSTANDING HIS CONTRIBUTIONS

It wasn't until about a year ago, when I met and became friends with Marcus Luttrell, that I was better able to put my experiences in Iraq in perspective. I said to him, "I was just a pilot." He said, "Look, not everybody is a Navy SEAL and went through what I went through. What you guys did was so important."

That meant a lot to me. I know what I experienced, but there was always this lingering sense that I wasn't kicking in doors and all that. But other than having our base taking mortar fire, I never really felt the kind of fear those other guys must have being in direct action.

I was pretty fearless at twenty-eight or twenty-nine, but I did feel vulnerable while in Iraq. I remember landing the aircraft and the base came under attack. A lot of times, we'd land or be in line for takeoff and we'd have to stop and sit there. I remember just sitting there and thinking, "Boy, I'm going to take one of those mortar rounds right here in the cockpit." But that never really worried me. Even when flying and my weapons alert alarm went on signaling an incoming missile, I was able to keep calm. I was more worried for the guys on the ground.

Unfortunately, I saw firsthand the negative effects that combat can have on individuals. A few buddies from the air force struggled post-deployment. More so, I saw the lingering effects of combat on my grandfather, Harry Kinzinger.

APPRECIATING HISTORY

I didn't know a lot about my grandfather's service history. We were told that he was in the Army Air Corps in World War II. He'd share a few stories, but mostly I remember being told not to play war around

Grandpa. My dad told me that he had memories of grandpa hiding under tables when low-flying aircraft came over the farmhouse. That was kind of hard for me to imagine. Grandpa Kinzinger was about six feet three, a huge farm dude. He came back from war and went to work right away on the family farm in Gilman, Illinois. He was pretty stoic.

When I decided to join the air force, we were having our family Thanksgiving dinner in 2002. I let him know what I was doing. I asked him if he could share a little of what he went through. Everyone else had left the table, and he said he'd try. He told me that he'd done some training in Florida but couldn't remember for how long. Then he said that he was over in France and that it was really, really cold. They had to keep the tanks rolling, and he started crying. I didn't press him for any more than that.

Growing up, he was always an inspiration to me. He died in 2003, during the invasion of Iraq. I thought about him a lot and what he experienced. When I left active duty and came back stateside, I went through an adjustment period. I was a pilot and didn't see anything at all like what he must have experienced as a forward observer. For him, and for every World War II veteran, it was like, "Thanks for being a part of the war. Great. Now go raise a family." And that's what he did. But he went back to the farm, and his head must have been ringing. I always think about that and what they went through. They didn't have near the kinds of services available to them that we do.

I see it another way now. I did, and still do, admire his stoicism, his silence. But I also see it as a kind of defect in him not being able to talk about and share and be open about his experiences. There are flaws in every man. He was great to us as kids. He didn't brag. He went and did his duty. He put it all on the line. I wondered if maybe he could have eased his suffering if he was able to talk about his experiences.

A NEW WAY FORWARD

At the beginning of 2020, I was thinking that this was the best time to be alive. Yet everybody seems more miserable than they've ever been. I was also thinking that maybe we needed another 9/11-type event to wake us all up. Well, this pandemic is a 9/11 moment, and we aren't waking up. People are becoming even more partisan.

The virus itself is partisan. The reaction to what we should do with China is partisan. I don't believe that we should use China as a political weapon.

The contempt I often see among the American people, quite honestly, fueled me to stay in this job longer. After ten years, you always evaluate. I do it every time I run. *Am I the right guy at the right time?* This thing has refueled me. My desire isn't to go out there and whack the Democrats on it. They'll whack us and we'll whack them, but nothing will change.

I want to inspire people again. I want them to look at the contempt in their heart. It comes from fear. Don't be afraid. Fear leads to conflict. Conflict leads to destroyed societies.

WE CAN BE DIFFERENT

My mission as a congressman is to restore a sense of what it means to be an American. Our pride. Our unity. And that doesn't mean a unity of beliefs. We each have different beliefs. And that's how it should be. I have a strong legislative agenda, but from a large perspective, I want to restore unity in this country. We can be a source of inspiration and light. I also want to be sure that we continue our mission around the world. Now is not the time to withdraw. Now is the time for us to step forward and lead.

What goes through my head daily is my experience in the military. The vast majority of air force pilots I worked with were Republicans. I flew with a few Democrats and in our off hours we'd talk politics and argue. But at that moment in time, we were all on that mission together. And at that moment in time, our mission was to defend our country. It wasn't, *Is Obama going to get elected or is John McCain?* It was the mission of the country that mattered.

In Congress, I know that you should keep your partisan lines to some extent. That's what the people who elected you want. But you also have to be willing to work on things together. The tone you take is what really makes a difference.

And in a crisis, I can fall back on my pilot training. We were taught that no matter the emergency, just stop, take a breath, analyze the situation. More specifically, we're told, "Maintain aircraft control, analyze the situation, take appropriate action, and land as soon as conditions permit." The same is true with anything in life. Maintain control. Keep your emotions in check.

WE CAN BE BETTER THAN WE THINK

That training took on real-world implications in 2006. I was home after flying border missions with the Air National Guard, drove up to Milwaukee with a friend and the woman I was dating at the time.

It was 12:26 a.m. A woman came running across North Avenue in Milwaukee. She was holding her throat and it was clear to me that she was bleeding heavily. The first thing that went through my mind was that this was some kind of early Halloween prank. It was August, but still that was my initial thought. A moment later, a man came running after her, holding a knife. He was covered in blood.

No, I thought. *This is real.*

The woman staggered up to us.

I had two distinct thoughts.

If I fight him, I might die.

I can't watch this happen, do nothing, and then live with myself later.

I started yelling for someone to help me. I yelled at my girlfriend to take the injured woman away and get her in a car. I tried to calm the guy down. He just stared blankly at me, clearly out of it. He wasn't going to listen to reason, so I switched tactics and started cursing at him. I figured if he got mad enough at me, he'd leave the woman alone and I could run away faster than she could.

He stepped around me and tried to drag the woman from out of the car, trying to stab her.

I don't have a clear memory of this part, but I do know that I grabbed his knife hand and wrapped my arm around his neck. He was much bigger and stronger than me, and I could feel his arm coming down at me with the knife in his hand.

That's it. I'm done. I'm going to die.

Somehow, I got him on the ground. I had made the decision to kill him. I'm a huge concealed carry advocate because of situations like this. I wasn't armed, but the police showed up a few seconds later.

The lesson I learned from that is you learn what you're capable of. They always taught us in the military that if you are in a situation where somebody walks into a room with a gun, half the people in that room will run, 40 percent will freeze because they want to act but don't know how and they can't think. Ten percent of people will take over and tell other people what to do.

You need to be able to take action. To do something. Take control. My father worked for a few different faith-based organizations. My mom was a teacher. They instilled in me the idea that you need to be of service. That situation in Milwaukee was an extreme case, but

I see in it how a lot of the choices I made in life all came together to help that woman out. She survived. Her attacker, believe it or not, is already out of jail. Maybe I should be afraid that he'll come after me. That's a legitimate form of fear. So was the fear I felt that night when we were wrestling over that knife.

What I don't see as being as legitimate is the kind of fear that seems to be gripping a lot of people in this country. If you're on the right of the political spectrum, you're afraid that the country you love has changed. You're afraid that you're being left behind. You're afraid that those on the other side are going to create a system of government that oppresses you.

On the left, you also fear that you're going to be left behind. You fear that you're not being included. You fear that we have a government that is of, for, and by only a select few.

In fact, I think both sides share that fear.

The reality is, that fear is unfounded. It's not true. The most liberal Democrat and entrenched Republican have the same goal in mind—success and happiness.

We differ on how to get there. And the 24-hour-a-day social media, the 24-hour-a-day news media, feed those fears. Fear has become an addiction.

The way to combat that is to take a deep breath and analyze the situation. What are you afraid of?

I'm afraid that the Democrats are going to win the election.

Why does that frighten you?

Because they are going to do X, Y, and Z.

And what's so scary about those possibilities?

Finally, if you drill down deep enough, you'll get to your base fear and hopefully you'll realize that it is unfounded.

There's a spiritual component to this as well. I give up my fear to God and I trust him. But if you're not a spiritual person, you have to be able to understand your fear, where it springs from, and what steps you can take to deal with it. But if you allow yourself to become addicted to the fear then you enter into a cycle of anger and outrage. Man, that cycle shortens lives and makes people miserable. It's corrosive.

PURPOSE AND POSITIVITY

Fear operates best in an environment of uncertainty. As I said, when I was younger, I doubted that I could be a pilot. Through my military training and my pilot training, I developed a belief in myself and in my capabilities. I learned that I could take control and respond. That's what I hope to do for the American people. I want them to believe in themselves. I want them to be able to dispel fear. I want them to be real.

One of the things I've learned since being in Congress is that it is a lot more important to listen than to be heard. I understand better how to deal with people. I now want to hear both sides. When I was first elected, I would speak up every time I could because I thought that what I had to say was so important. That's not always the case. Whenever I do get attention for things I've said, it's because I spoke from my heart and didn't recite talking points. When I say what I believe and am real with the people I'm talking to, they respect me more.

I'm fortunate that I'm a veteran and no one ever really questions my credibility on veterans' issues. But I see this country trying to make veterans victims. You come back from serving, you get a pat on the head, you're given a good paycheck for a disability if you were wounded, and then you're told to go fishing for the rest of your life. And only veterans can address some of the problems we have within the system.

And veterans need to be held accountable, too. When I was running for Congress in '09, I spoke to a Disabled Veterans of America group. Someone came up to me and asked me what my disability rating was. I told him that I didn't really know, maybe 10 percent for my neck and more for a few other minor issues. He told me, "That's only about 30 percent. I can get you to 70 percent." I stood there thinking that this is not how this system is supposed to work. We shouldn't be gaming it to get as much as we can unless we deserve it. I know of veterans who've lost a leg and receive a 70 percent disability payment. Should you be getting that if you have ringing in your ears and sleep issues? No.

Most of us went into the military because we wanted to be a part of a mission that is greater than ourselves. That's why I think you see so many honorable people coming out of the military. For the most part, for the vast majority of veterans, you get treated fairly in the military. When you take into account all the benefits you receive, you're being paid fairly. That should continue after you're done serving.

This country needs to quit writing all these checks to veterans and start encouraging them to make the best of their life ahead. That's another mission I have in Congress: to give veterans purpose.

I know what it is like to come out of active duty service. All of a sudden, you're spit out into civilian life. It's hard. I went through it. Even though I ran for Congress immediately and had a goal in mind, I still struggled. For the first four years in Congress I thought about resigning and going back into the air force full time. It was great to be elected, but the proudest days of my life were when I earned my wings and when I became a lieutenant colonel. Nothing really compares with the sense of accomplishment you get from serving your country. That doesn't mean you can't find another mission to take on. If that means going back to working on a farm like my granddad did, then do that fiercely. If it means doing some other kind of work then do that.

It's all about the end of your life. What can you say you did? What was your life worth? What did you contribute?

We don't all have to go in the military, but we can all make America a better place.

That's the aspect of life today, especially in politics, that really troubles me. We're experiencing a real breakdown in appreciation for each other and all the ways we contribute to our collective betterment. That's what drives me. I've been around the world and seen situations far worse than our own.

I've also seen some of our modern warriors come back from war, and I admire their efforts to show people again what life is about. Just like in the Bible, they were willing to enact violence to protect the people they love. Then they come back, pass on lessons, and inspire a new generation to bigger things.

CHAPTER 10

LIEUTENANT (RET.)
MORGAN LUTTRELL

UNITED STATES NAVY

There's a resiliency in guys like us. For me, I believe it stems from a lot of failures in life. I got tired of losing and getting my ass kicked. Eventually I convinced myself if somebody else could do it, then why couldn't I.

We'd been rehearsing vessel-borne search and seizure (VBSS) drills all day, and now we were into nighttime. Earlier, we'd reviewed the conditions. We were the helo assault force (HAF) being flown by the army's 160th, the most elite rotary wing asset in the US arsenal. The weather and sea state were taking a turn for the worse, but in our community, the harsher the conditions the better. The call was made, and we were going!

Fast roping is exactly that—fast. You have to be out of the bird and on the deck in seconds. We'd done it all day, but this time, the winds were bad, and the sea state was worse, and it was taking minutes. When I looked out the door, I noticed the rotors were inches from the boat. Then sugar turned to absolute shit: I heard metal on metal, the bird pitched sideways, and we were closing on the deck, helo and all, free-falling from about forty feet. Kitted up, you can add sixty to eighty pounds to my usual 220. I hit the deck on my ass, felt everything go, and I made that stupid sound you make when all the air rushes out of your body. I laid there stunned for a second before I felt the explosion's concussive effects lifting me up and tossing me down to a lower deck. I fell another ten to twenty feet and landed on my head. I don't remember a whole lot after that.

★★

Morgan Luttrell sometimes jokingly introduces himself as Marcus Luttrell's brother. There's truth to that. He and Marcus are twins, born in the Houston area. He is a sixth-generation Texan. Most every male in his family has served in the military. The family has traced its lineage back and determined that one member of the family has served in every war that America has been involved in, as well many in Europe before the family emigrated to America.

Hard work was a way of life on a horse ranch, and Morgan is proud and grateful to be the first person in his family to graduate from college, earning a degree in psychology and philosophy from Sam Houston State University. Luttrell enlisted in the navy, graduating BUD/S with class 237. After serving as a SEAL for seven years, Luttrell attended Officer Candidate School, after which he became a commissioned officer with Naval Special Warfare.

Morgan retired from the military during his fourteenth year of service with multiple deployments in support of the war on terror. After retirement, he went on to pursue an advanced degree in applied cognition and neuroscience at the University of Texas at Dallas and graduated with honors, which set a strong foundation for him to support his military brothers and first responders. He has served as the CEO for Boot Campaign, a nonprofit veteran-assistance program providing a comprehensive and individualized approach to increasing the mental and physical well-being of America's military and first-responding heroes. The program employs the expertise from facilities like the Center for Brain Health at the University of Texas at Dallas, where Luttrell served as a research scientist after graduating. In 2017 Luttrell received his appointment to the Department of Energy as senior adviser to the secretary.

He recently completed his executive education at Harvard Business School, focused on professional leadership development. Luttrell resides in Texas with his wife and two sons.

★★

TURNING A BAD BREAK INTO A BREAKTHROUGH

Morgan Luttrell sustained multiple injuries that had him in a body cast for several months following that 2009 training incident. The crash and explosion resulted in the loss of one life and serious injuries to eight service members. Morgan believes that he was one of the lucky ones—despite him breaking his back in multiple places and suffering a severe traumatic brain injury.

I was post-concussive for two months after that. I don't remember anything from that time frame. People would later tell me that they came by the house to see me, told me about what we did, but I had no clue about that.

I am grateful for many things related to that crash, but the most important lesson I learned is that no matter how good your contingency plan is, things are going to happen that you can't predict. That night, though, everyone on the team came together and did the right thing and saved lives. My teammates crawled into the burning wreckage and pulled the injured out of the fire.

I'm also thankful that my physical injuries were treated by some of the finest doctors and rehabilitation specialists around the country. Months later, I was back making a deployment with the same platoon, a testament to the amazing advances in science and technology. I feel very lucky that those I served with began to notice some differences in my capabilities caused by my TBI. My body was sound, but my cognitive abilities were not.

My deficits were subtle. Things like I wouldn't complete a sentence in an email. I'm pretty articulate and a good writer, but I could no longer put my thoughts to paper and make it make sense. I was submitting things where a sentence just ended right in the middle.

Also, I was getting absent-minded. I'd walk into a room and then ask myself, *Why did I come in here?* or *Where was I going?* Sometimes it would take someone asking me a specific question about a task I was working on for me to check back in on my status.

I'd worked extremely hard to get back to the physical level that I was at before the crash, but I didn't really notice any of the cognitive issues I had until someone pointed them out to me. Once they noticed a trend, I started to document more examples of them. That's when I knew I needed help to get back to being the mental Morgan that I was before.

I was both an operator and an officer. I tried to reset my baseline. I had to be as sharp as possible—I needed to have everything working up top to execute both those roles.

The navy had never performed any neurological assessments or baseline scans on my brain, MRI, CT, DTI, etc. . . . Before I was injured, the body, yes, extensively, thoroughly; my head, not so much. The reason, I'm guessing, is because it wasn't common practice at that time. Months after my accident I searched out the premier doctors and institutions of cognitive and physical health in order to build a complete diagnostic portfolio on exactly what was going on with me. After the testing was complete, I sat with my doctors and formulated the best way to correct the issues I was having.

I worked with clinicians, neurologists, neuroscientists, nutritionists, psychologists, dieticians, and exercise physiologists. I knew that I had to fix my brain and body at the same time. Fixing one without the other seemed pointless. I can't take my head off at night and put it on the bedside table. They work together in harmony, one fluid machine, and ignoring one would drastically limit my chances of a full recovery. Looking at the images of my brain, I wanted to know, "What particular area of the brain does this part of the scan or assessment test for?" They told me, "Well, that's reasoning." All right, well, my reasoning sucks. So how do I fix that? With their help, I started inundating my brain with reasoning exercises, with reasoning questions and scenarios. "How do you decrease symptomatic issues when one presents itself?" And so on and so forth.

On to the next problem to fix.

All right, what's this particular one? Well, this is memory recall. Okay, my memory recall is shot. How do I fix that? Well, we have to do memory recall testing and focused assessments. And I would work on cognitive development exercises. I took them on deployment with me. Other people would read and watch TV and play video games. I would do my brain development exercises and other work, because I wanted my head to be back where it needed to be.

It's like a rehabilitation routine for somebody who has broken a bone, broken a leg. You're going to get in the gym and rehab that leg. You have to rehab your brain. People get frustrated with it because it's boring and it sucks. But I didn't think that way. I wanted to do that for myself. And that's how I brought myself back.

I was in a leadership role. I was trying to get back to baseline. I had to be as sharp as possible—I needed to have everything working up top to execute that role effectively.

I want to make it clear that there is a huge difference between cognitive instabilities and post-traumatic stress. I don't have post-traumatic stress. I spent my entire career giving that shit to other people. What I had was cognitive disabilities or distractions. And that was just because of the injury itself, and my brain hadn't properly healed itself to bring me back up to where I needed to be. I came in too fast. I got back too fast. And you have to give the brain time to heal. You really have to take an all-stop—no electronics, no light, no sugars, no stimulation of any kind if possible. Just let the brain start to heal itself and give it the time, like you would a bone. We don't do that because we want to be with the team, in the mix. We need to be on the line.

After I graduated from the University of Texas at Dallas with a master's degree in cognition and neuroscience I went to work with the Department of Energy. At one point, we had a meeting with NFL commissioner Roger Goodell about how the DOE could assist and run simulations on TBIs and possible chronic traumatic encephalopathy (CTE) outcomes and how the two correlate. This was when the NFL was really starting to get into concussion and CTE issues.

This was extremely challenging. In the veterans' space, it's not usually known that a veteran committed suicide because of CTE that was caused by TBIs.

Is it a bigger deal than when a veteran kills himself or herself? No, absolutely not. But these football players are our heroes. They are the ones we watch on Saturday and Sunday; we follow their careers. When an NFL veteran kills himself, we all wonder, *Why would they do that?* They didn't see war. They don't have post-traumatic stress. What's going on here?

Veterans with cognitive and emotional issues are often diagnosed with PTSD. They may be receiving or have received treatment for PTSD, but those treatments aren't effective because those treatments may not be addressing the underlying cause. Very often, these guys sustained undiagnosed TBIs. Unless they are diagnosed with TBIs and receive the proper treatment, other treatments are just a Band-Aid, masking the underlying cause, or creating other problems like addiction and suicide.

After my accident, I came out of the hospital on seven different narcotics, five of them opioids. Luckily, I ran out on a holiday and couldn't fill the prescriptions. I detoxed over the weekend, went cold turkey, and never took a narcotic after that.

What the NFL is doing to address concussion issues and CTE is really important. These are our heroes on the field. We can use the attention their brain injuries receive to put a focus on the injuries that our heroes on the battlefield sustain. Hopefully, we can use the combined research to more effectively diagnose and treat our veterans.

When I was downrange and active, I rarely saw PTSD. Even if anybody had it, I didn't see it. When you're in the tribe, you're so close to one another you see when a guy's having issues. You rally around him and help him out of that hole. When we leave that tribe, that's when problems start to manifest. They don't have that support structure anymore. They're not around people who speak their language anymore and understand them. I would love to see our veteran community shifting from their roles in active duty to continuing to serve veterans after they separate. The American public needs to understand that veterans are dynamic and educated individuals coming out of the military that may need some guidance. I want my veteran brothers and sisters to understand that civilians may not understand you. That's not their fault. Be patient.

Morgan's physical injuries took a greater toll on him later, and after fourteen years, he retired. In visiting various cognitive rehabilitation clinics around the country, he found a new passion—neuroscience. That's when he pursued advanced degrees in that field. That's why he's committed to helping other veterans and their families understand how TBIs can sometimes produce elusive effects and how allowing the brain enough time to heal properly is so essential.

Morgan has worked tirelessly to champion various veterans' causes, but none is more important to him than educating others about the brain.

LEARNING THE HARD WAY

"I was sitting on the couch with Marcus one day when we were maybe thirteen, and a Discovery Channel program about Navy SEALs came on. I'll never forget it. It changed my life. The narrator was talking about the covert operations the SEALs took part in all over the world. Marcus and I were outdoorsy. We loved swimming and running around in the woods playing Rambo. This was before Charlie Sheen and *Navy SEALs* came out. Man, watching that show, the hair on the back of my neck stood up. I looked over at my brother and said, 'Hey, we're going to be SEALs!'"

Part of our effort to make that dream come true was working with a nearby veteran named Billy "Soupbone" Shelton. I went to school with Soupbone's daughter and had known him all his life. He had earned a reputation in the area for having trained successful candidates for the SEALs, Green Berets, and other Special Forces units.

Billy would always say how proud he was to help guys like Marcus and me. He was proud that a new generation of kids was willing to do what it took to defend the country like his generation had. He was serious about that, and if you didn't live up to his standards, he'd tighten the screws on us. "You sons of bitches need to remember that you are going out there to defend every single person that lives in this country. If you're not going to put out right here in this yard, what makes you think you can put out in your SEAL teams." He'd send us home if we weren't performing to his high standards. That hurt, but it always made us want to come back.

Because of the mental duress he put us under, I was able to endure everything I went through in training. A lot of guys train physically but they don't do the mental and emotional work. With Billy, when we were working with him, he was our worst enemy. When we were done, when we'd done well, he was our best friend.

A severe leg injury almost delayed my entry into BUD/S. I almost wasn't able to get into the navy at all. The injury required surgery that I couldn't afford. I remember lying on my couch, sweating from the pain. I'd busted my foot, my ankle, and had a tibia-fibula fracture. I was messed up. I needed plates and screws but had no money for the procedure. The surgery center waived their fees, but the anesthesiologist didn't. I needed $700. A friend came up with the cash for me. Unfortunately, the navy wouldn't honor my delayed entry agreement that was going to get me into BUD/S. Not with a messed-up leg like I had. Marcus was in BUD/S at the time, and he got a doctor to look me over and give me a waiver. I'd healed up by then, done a ton of rehab work, but with those plates and screws in there, I could have been rejected. I went back to the recruiting station in Houston and showed them my paperwork and I was told I was good to go. I was able to graduate from SEAL training as the class honor man.

I came from a small town. I always believed that SEALs were these superhumans who were created in a lab from some top-secret genetic code. In my mind they were Olympic-level athletes and I was just a guy from BFE Texas who grew up shoveling horseshit. At BUD/S we started with 250 guys, and twenty-seven originals graduated. That's when I learned that if some other guy could do it, so could I.

BUD/S training was as difficult as advertised and then some. But as tough as it was, I draw on those lessons all the time. I'll never forget the experience. On one training operation, we went past insanity. We were underwater for seven hours in 39-degree water. I went deeper in a hole than I did during any time during Hell Week. During that dive, if I could have, I would have probably tried to kill myself. When we got done, I came out of the water and the rest of the team and me sat around and laughed. "Man, that sucked."

But we all had something worse to compare that experience with. For me that was a time when I had to go down into a literal hole during BUD/S. In a group of approximately eighty other candidates, we had to dig a hole in the beach large enough to conceal ourselves. Then we had to get inside it and avoid detection. As one of the bigger guys, I had to lie at the bottom. I figured that was good. No one could see me, so they couldn't beat on me. I forgot one thing. How much seventy-nine grown men weigh and that urine flows downhill.

After an hour in that pile, we were eventually instructed to leave the hole, get wet, cover ourselves in sand, and put our uniforms back on. Only we couldn't take time to put on our own clothes. We had to grab from a pile and put on whatever we could get our hands on in two minutes. If even one of us wasn't dressed in that time limit, then it was back in the water. I wound up wearing clothes so small it was like I was wearing capri pants and a crop-top T-shirt.

I fell to my knees, weeping into my hands. I'd never been that cold, wet, tired, and miserable before. I wasn't thinking of quitting; I was just having a moment.

One of my class officers walked up to me and hit me on the shoulder. "Hey, Luttrell, what's going on?"

"Sir, that's the most awful night I've had in my entire life. I've never been . . . it was horrible."

"Goddamn, son, that was last night. It's morning now; the sun's up. That shit's over. Let's grab some chow."

I tell people all the time that I learned a life lesson at that moment. I knew that we were all going to be put in a hole, a real one, a figurative one—at some point. You're always told, *Don't get into a hole, and if you do, stop digging when you're in there.* What we learned was that we could go into that hole and come out of it and keep going. We had to prove to ourselves, to America, that we could do that.

APPLYING THE LESSONS TO LIFE

Somebody told me a long time ago that there's rational and irrational fear. You have to be able to differentiate between the two. Rational fear's a good thing. Irrational fear will get you killed, and you have to be able to put that out of your mind. Rational fear keeps you sharp, keeps you focused, keeps you pointed, keeps you driven. It allows your muscle memory to react.

So you are fearful sometimes. It works like this: You ask yourself, *Am I possibly going to get hurt or lose my life?* Yes. But that's okay: That's what I signed up for. That's why it's a voluntary program. And the sons of bitches on my left and right? They're thinking the exact same thing. So then I'm going. I miss that. When you're moving out, going outside the wire on an operation, every sense is heightened. You notice everything. If you don't, well, then that's when bad things can happen.

KEEPING IT SIMPLE

When people want to know what it's like to see combat, I tell them, "You don't want to know and you won't get it anyway." It's the best and worst of humanity all in one, all at the same time. For me, a warrior is somebody who volunteers for conflict. Warriors embrace the old ways, the code. We live for the struggle, the adversity, the hardship, and the misery. For me, someone who joined the military to be a part of a warrior culture, I knew that it was not if, but when. I knew I was going to get hurt or I might die. It didn't matter. That's what I signed up for. I literally signed up to blow shit up and kill bad people. Luckily for me, there was a war going on and I could do that. I was doing a two-mile swim in BUD/S when 9/11 happened—that was the worst and the best day all at once. There isn't a day that goes by in my life that I don't wish I was back there fighting.

The effects of combat touch more than just two dudes going at it. If you take a life or lose one, you're also having an effect on that family. You killed or lost a husband/wife, a brother/sister, a mother/father. And those effects keep rippling. How far? Who knows? From start to finish I maintained the idea that I was there to rid the planet of very bad people. I wanted to get the ones who were creating havoc and fear and were preying on others.

For certain duty, honor, politics, and all the rest, there's none of that in a gunfight. I promise you that. The people you're after do not care if you're a Republican or a Democrat. If somebody's trying to kill you, they don't care if you're patriotic. They don't care what state you're from. None of that.

And all of that taught me an important lesson. Don't be petty. Never. Never. Never. I grew up in a small town, in the country, and I went on to serve with the greatest men and women in the military. I went into combat and fought next to those people. I lost some of those people. Now, today, I see so much petty shit that people get wrapped up in and hassle one another over. I don't care if you're talking about race, religion, politics—whatever. It's just so petty.

There's a civil war going on in our country between the red and blue. I worked in Washington, DC, for a while, in the government, and I walked into a few rooms, and I could tell some people actually hated me because I worked for the Trump administration. I was in the business of saving lives, helping veterans and their families, informing people about the necessity to understand the difference between PTSD and TBIs. Still, politics got in the way of me delivering an important message.

I try to walk right down the middle of the red and blue divide. My team and I just wanted to help people. There was just so much that was bad and ugly in DC. That was so ridiculous. I almost got killed a bunch of times, and saw too many teammates die, for it to be like this.

If people in government, in the media, in the general public were to actually listen to and value the opinions of veterans about what the hell is going on, then we'd stop sweating all this small stuff. I wish everyone realized how lucky we are to live in this country and have the opportunities we do. If you think you've got it bad here, go to some of the places I've been and see how bad those people have it.

All that said, there was a time when I was petty. It took me five years after I retired to truly be out of the navy. The military does a very good job of bringing people in, breaking them down, creating what it wants them to be, what we need, and what we have to have. They create a precision instrument. They do that really well. But what it does poorly is offloading that precision instrument and putting it back into the private sector. That is the space that I live in now, trying to provide proper guidance to those coming out of the military. It's like our military personnel are on a bullet train, and it barely slows down when it comes time to let our people off when they leave the service. I was fortunate. I had someplace to land—graduate school—and from there I could figure out what my next play was.

But even with that advantage, I was angry. Just pissed off. I was in class, and I'd look around the classroom at all these people younger than me who'd never done anything with their lives except sit in a classroom. Funny thing was, this was in an ethics class, and we had to talk about a lot of deep shit, and I'd done my share of facing real-world issues. Those other kids were saying things I thought were just about the dumbest, most naïve crap I'd ever heard.

Then I had an epiphany. I realized that I was the one who was different. They couldn't help but be who they were, and think the way they did, because of the things they'd experienced that had shaped them. I knew then that I couldn't be hard on those kids. I shouldn't judge them. What if somebody had done that to me? Hell, it took me six years to get an undergraduate degree and I did it with a 2.01 grade point average. I think I was number 760 out of 760 in my graduating class. Yet I graduated from my master's program with a 3.9 GPA. I'm not the same man I was twenty years ago. I didn't have that drive, that direction, that discipline.

And all that change is because of my military experience. I don't think that many outside those who've been through the kinds of training and tests we go through can appreciate just how transformative it can be. That's part of the reason why I believe that we need more veterans helping other veterans solve their problems. We speak the same language, a language that very few civilians understand. Veterans are going to have to step up. We're going to have to be the neuroscientists and psychologists finding effective treatments for PTSD, TBIs, depression, and suicide. We're going to have to become the CEOs, founders, and others in positions of power in private industry to lead and to teach others to understand the value of the veteran community's skill sets. I think we can solve these problems. For hundreds of years, the military has had a 99.9 percent success rate. We win.

We don't always do that in the veteran community now, but we will.

CHAPTER 11

CAPTAIN (RET.)
SEAN PARNELL
UNITED STATES ARMY

People have been telling
me all my life that I can't do
things. And I've always used
that as, *Okay, all right, I got
it. You're a naysayer, you're
a critic, and that's going to
be my motivation to do it.*

---

ission first. Men always." That's always been the infantry's creed. That was on my mind when I got to my unit in 2005. We were infantrymen, members of the 10th Mountain Division, and my platoon, officially the 3rd, was known as the Outlaws.

We were thrown into the meat grinder, man. We didn't really know what we were getting ourselves into. If you remember the news cycle in 2005, everybody was talking about the surge, right? The surge and weapons of mass destruction, the debate about the "failed" Iraq war was raging on Capitol Hill. And because of that, the eyes of this nation were not focused on the Afghan war. In fact, most people thought it was just a stability and support operation and that the war had already been won.

And as an infantry unit, we did everything that we thought we should be doing that would prep us for deployment to combat. We ran a lot of miles and banged lots of cadence and shot a lot of bullets. We really did everything that we could to shoot, move, and communicate together as a team. But when we got to Afghanistan, you realized that once that first bullet cracks by your head, you hope that the training that you did leading up to that was good. But man, we weren't expecting the level of enemy resistance in Afghanistan that we eventually faced.

And man, we were in thousands of . . . I feel like over four thousand indirect fire attacks on our base, over four thousand in a 485-day period. Hundreds. Hundreds. Almost every day we left the wire, we were in a direct fire engagement with the enemy. We took an 85 percent casualty rate. Some men were wounded twice. I was wounded myself. Six of my men were shot in the head. All of them survived by the grace of God, I think, alone.

★★★★★★★★★★★★★★★★★★★★★★★★★★★★★★★★★★★★

In a typical display of humility, Captain Sean Parnell underplays his own role within the Outlaw Platoon. Under his leadership, it would become one of the most fierce and effective fighting units in modern times. It also is still one of the most highly decorated units since 9/11, and was responsible for taking out more than 350 enemy fighters.

Also, Sean wasn't just wounded in a June 10, 2006, firefight; he was knocked unconscious and wounded two more times. Despite that, he got back up and led his men again. As one of his men later put it, "Sean Parnell saved us all." Still on the battlefield, Sean suffered from his untreated head wounds for weeks. Cerebrospinal fluid leaked from his ears and nose, but he continued to go with his men outside the wire. His tenacity came at a cost. When he returned from that deployment, he was forced to medically discharge from the army. He later went on to recount the remarkable accomplishments of the men he led in the *New York Times* bestseller *Outlaw Platoon*.

Born and raised in Pittsburgh, Pennsylvania, he is the oldest of four children. Sean has said that he struggled in school, was bullied terribly, and once had an elementary school teacher say to him in front of the entire class that he was never going to reach the standards of his engineer father. "She said that in front of my Italian American mother, and that was a big mistake." Sean was placed in classes with other kids with learning disabilities, but he saw his academic issues as more of a lack of focus.

He found that focus when his parents decided to transfer him from the local public high school to Greensburg Central Catholic High School. "There was something about having my faith and my education united that gave me a sense of purpose. In a way, that was my rocket fuel and gave me a mission."

That mission would eventually see him attend Clarion University for a while before transferring to Duquesne University so that he could also enroll in its Reserve Officer Training Corps. That eventually led to him being a part of the legendary 10th Mountain Division, serving with distinction for six years, and retiring as a captain who was awarded two Bronze Stars, one with Valor; and the Purple Heart.

Sean continues to serve with distinction. As of the writing of this book, he is running to represent Pennsylvania's Seventeenth District in our nation's House of Representatives. Should he win, he'll be a newly minted freshman congressman in January 2021. Before running for Congress, he helped advocate for the 2014 legislation that eventually became known as the Mission Act. He also worked tirelessly on the 2015 VA Accountability Act. He co-founded the American Warrior Initiative, an organization to support our veterans. He lives in Ohio Township, Pennsylvania, with his three children.

★★★★★★★★★★★★★★★★★★★★★★★★★★★★★★★★★★★★★★★

This was back at a time when traumatic brain injury, TBI, wasn't even an acronym. Guys were getting shot in the head, and because they didn't want to let one another down, they'd bandage up their heads and go right back out on patrol. It was the most inspirational thing I had ever seen in my life, and that's where I learned a very profound leadership lesson: as a young leader going into the military, you always hear that great leaders are supposed to inspire their troops, but the truth is that when lives are on the line and the rubber meets the road, great troops inspire their leaders. And these kids, man, they inspired me to fight harder than I ever thought possible.

God, man, when I tell you that we were the most diverse infantry unit that you could possibly imagine, I really do mean it. Black, white, Asian, Latino, all in the same foxhole. Christian, Muslim, atheist, Jewish, all in the same foxhole. Six of my men weren't even citizens of this country. Someone from Mexico; someone from South Vietnam; someone from Haiti; someone from Murmansk, Russia. All these guys were in my platoon, and they just all came to this country because they loved it, they believed we were an exceptional nation, and they wanted to serve.

And I watched these guys. We weren't Navy SEALs or Special Operators. Don't get me wrong, we had some really cool, sexy training, but we were just light infantry men. The job of these kids before they were toting a gun through the mountains of Afghanistan was, in most cases, like high school shortstop. I saw them perform just one feat, one triumph of the human spirit after the next in Afghanistan. And really, we learned very clearly that yeah, we've got better weapons than the enemy and cooler technology, but our secret weapon over there was the love and brotherhood that we had for one another as Americans, as American war fighters. And ultimately, that love and brotherhood that we had with one another was what allowed us to survive that horrific deployment.

After, I think, four months in country, we made a promise to each other, a pact after a big firefight where we were almost overrun, but we said, "We're not going to ever cede an inch to the enemy. We will stand and fight, regardless of how bad things get." Because earlier that month, we had seen, coming back to the base, an infantry battalion who broke contact and ran after an ambush. And the look in the eyes of those men—they were just devastated psychologically.

They didn't want to ever leave the wire again. And we didn't want that for our troops. So we said, "We're going to stand and fight," and so we did.

We were about as diverse as you can imagine, but there were no hyphenated Americans in our platoon. We were all just Americans. We were all galvanized behind one mission, fighting for a common purpose. Because of that, we were able to accomplish incredible things. So I think, and I've been saying time and time again, on both sides of the aisle, we'll learn a lot of things when the dust settles from this pandemic. But one of the lessons that I hope we take away is just how important leadership really, truly is. That's what I'm hoping to bring to the fight in Congress. But we do live in an extraordinarily divided time, and it's going to be up to the next generation of leaders to heal that divide and do everything we can to bring Americans together.

One of the primary messages of my campaign is that when Americans are united, we can accomplish anything. When Americans were united, we sent a man to the moon. We won the space race with less technology than we're utilizing today when we talk on the phone.

I say all the time I'm running for Congress as a leader, and leaders bring people together. They focus on our commonality. They don't focus on our differences. And as Americans, we have far more things that unite us than divide us. A lot of people say, "Oh, diversity is our greatest strength," but I think that misses a core component. Diversity is a great strength, but the reason why our diversity in Afghanistan in Outlaw Platoon was a great strength is because we put aside our differences and we united in spite of the differences.

A GALVANIZING MOMENT

Sean's life mission didn't come into immediate focus even after he persisted in overcoming his childhood academic challenges and attended Clarion University. He struggled there, again feeling as if he had no real direction in his life. On the morning of September 11, 2001, after a long night of partying at his off-campus apartment, Sean woke feeling queasy. He'd spent the evening with his roommates drinking beer and talking.

We were talking about how our generation didn't have a galvanizing moment that shaped our generation. We just really felt like we were living in a golden age. We were the middle children of that golden age. And I woke up in this rundown college apartment on this rundown college couch. I was lying on my back, looking at the ceiling. The room was spinning and there were beer cans littering the floor and cigarette butts everywhere. The whole apartment smelled like stale beer. I staggered over to the television and turned it on just in time to see a plane crash into the World Trade Center.

And at that moment, I was just really shaken to my core. I was afraid; I was angry. There was a lot of uncertainty at that time, and I remember staggering a few steps back and sitting on that rundown college couch for what felt like hours, just watching images of raw horror as they engulfed our fellow Americans, watching people tumble to their deaths from those flaming towers and land on the sidewalk and die on national TV. And the people that were lucky enough to survive that fateful day staggered out of the wreckage, covered from head to toe with thick, gray soot. Thick, gray soot; bloodshot eyes; and a thousand-yard stare.

Something that affected me in a really deep and profound way was the first responders just tirelessly working, day in and day out, to save lives. Instead of running away from the flames, I watched them run headlong into them. And then, with horror, watched the buildings collapse, knowing that everyone who ran into flames that day to try to save people, people that they didn't even know, had given their life. It was just something that . . . it was one of those moments that really . . . I don't know. I felt like my whole life was boiled down into those few moments after September 11. And I felt like, *Okay, I'm really at a crossroads here*. I could either continue down the path of this missionless college kid that didn't really know what he wanted to do with his life, or I could join the military and get in the fight and be a part of America's collective response.

And that's what I did. Two days later, I went down to the recruiter station. I told the recruiter that I wanted to join the infantry because I wanted to be on the front lines. And not only that, I wanted to go to Airborne School, where the army would teach me how to jump out of perfectly good airplanes. And not only that, I wanted to go to Ranger School because I knew it was the best leadership school that the army had to offer, and I wanted to be the best leader that I could for my troops. I just believed that with the US flag on your shoulder, and the might and power of the US military at your back, you can conquer the world. You could really accomplish any mission.

PERSISTENCE PAYS OFF

For Sean, it wasn't quite that simple. His decision met a bit of resistance from his father. Sean also learned something that he hadn't previously known—his father had dropped out of the United States Naval Academy at the same point Sean was thinking of leaving college—their sophomore year. His father's reason was also to serve—in this case, Sean's pregnant mother and ultimately him. Father and son came to a compromise: Sean transferred schools and entered the ROTC program. The battle to get into battle was delayed for a bit.

I progressed through the ROTC program with the intent of joining the infantry. And every waking moment of every single day was dedicated toward that goal. And you had to be at the top of your class to get it, because you're competing with a bunch of other cadets, and those cadets all want—for the most part—the infantry or some other type of high-speed training. So I had to make sure that I gave myself the best shot to get that selection. So that meant I had to be at the top of my class academically. That meant that I had to be at the top of my class militarily in the ROTC classes. And it meant I had to be top third at my advanced camp, which was out in Fort Lewis, Washington, which is the last camp that you do prior to your senior year in college.

I felt like I checked all those boxes. I even won the George C. Marshall Award, an ROTC leadership honor. I was thinking, *I'm going to be a shoo-in for infantry. It's going to be great.*

Then branch day came out, and I was assigned to Air Defense Artillery—my fourth choice. At that time, Air Defense Artillery was a dead branch. The army had just taken all of the short-range missiles out of the tactical infantry battalion, and SHARD, short-range air defense, was going away.

I was so pissed. I went to my battalion commander and I said, "Sir, what the hell? This is bullshit. I joined the military after 9/11 so I could get in the fight." And my battalion commander told me, "Well, they need good military officers in all the branches."

The army had just changed the process. Typically, if you're top third in everything and you bust your ass and you do what's right, you get your first choice. Well, that year they changed the accession rules. "We need good officers. We need a top-third officer in every branch." So they spread the wealth out a little bit. And I was pissed. "This is not what I signed up for." Like, if you raise your right hand and you volunteer to serve this country, you should be able to serve in the capacity that you want!

Bottom line is my protests all fell on deaf ears, but I wasn't done. I filled out what's called a 4187 branch transfer packet almost every other week. I graduated from school, and every week it was denied. And then I got my commission as a brand-new second lieutenant in the Air Defense Artillery. I was immediate active duty. I moved to Fort Bliss and started the Air Defense Artillery Officer Basic Course. And when I got there, every two weeks, I submitted a 4187 branch transfer packet to infantry, and every two weeks it would come back denied. And I said to myself, *Well, you know what, I don't care. I might not be where I want to be, but I'm still going to bust my ass to be the best that I can be.* And I ended up being one of the honor grads from the Air Defense Artillery Officer Basic Course. And again, through that twenty-week course, every two weeks I filled out that branch transfer packet, to no avail.

I went to Airborne School in November 2004 and graduated, still submitting my branch transfer packet even when I was there—no success. And I went home on leave for Christmas in December 2004, just crushed, thinking, *There's no way in hell I'm going to get what I want, but I'm going to submit one more packet.* So I did, and then I commenced drinking and eating Christmas cookies and letting myself get out of shape.

And the day before I was supposed to report to Fort Campbell, 2nd Battalion, 44th Air Defense Artillery—the day before!—

everything packed in our green army A bags and everything—I got a call saying, "Congratulations. Your branch transfer to infantry has been approved. Pack your bags. You're going to Ranger School." And I was like, *Well, shit. I just spent the last month drinking my ass off and eating Christmas cookies and I'm out of shape, and now I'm going to Ranger School.* And I'm like, *So I've gotten what I wanted, but be careful what you wish for.*

Those kinds of transfers never, ever happen. Mine did. I think I just annoyed everybody. It was like *Shawshank Redemption* where he writes the letters. I think they thought, *Please just stop writing to us!*

A SERIES OF VALUABLE LESSONS

Sean had to demonstrate even more tenacity in order to pass the army's most rigorous training program. With no infantry experience, he was definitely a fish out of water at Ranger School. Once downrange, his eyes were opened to another reality.

America's the greatest nation on the face of the earth, and this whole American experiment in individual freedom—or just freedom in general—is extraordinarily rare on the face of this earth. I went to Afghanistan, and this lesson was really driven home for me. You get to Afghanistan, and not only are you just struck by how primitive the country is—really, no electricity, no running water, no economy, nothing. I mean nothing. If you want to go back to a time where Jesus Christ walked the earth with an AK-47 in a pickup truck, that's Afghanistan. In fact, Jesus of Nazareth and his hometown were probably more advanced than portions of Afghanistan are today.

One of the things that struck me is the kids. They're running around in burlap sacks, covered from head to toe in filth, no socks, running through mountains on mountain rock, playing soccer with some deflated ball, just running around, smiling, happy, loving life. The kids in Afghanistan are no different than the kids here. And I just realized at that moment, watching those kids play soccer like that, that, man, they don't realize—they just love life. They're just like kids in America, except for not being blessed to be born in America and not in a war-torn country like Afghanistan.

Service to one's country does give you tremendous perspective on what is at stake should we lose the freedom that we have. Because in terms of freedom, America is the last best hope on earth. Nobody in the world has freedom like we do here; that's just the truth.

I always tell the next generation that life is about knocking on the door until your knuckles bleed. There's nothing easy about life. In fact, the road to unhappiness in life is paved with entitlement thinking. The fact of the matter is that nobody owes you anything.

And I think the antidote to most of life's issues is living life for others, living a life filled with service. The reason why you feel such a great sense of existential fulfillment as a military member is not only the band-of-brothers feeling, like you're serving with the greatest people in the world, you've got a mission that everyone's fighting for; but also, people forget: you're serving something greater than yourself. You're serving your country. You're putting your country before your family, before making a buck, before even maybe your life. And that service does give a sense of pride.

Only 0.4 percent of this country has raised their right hand and volunteered to serve in the longest period of war in our nation's history. Because service to the country is rare in this day and age, I came home, and in many ways, I felt like an exile in my own country. I did a welcome-home ceremony; I joined up with my family; there were big hugs and happy tears all around. But I couldn't help but feel that there was a barrier between my family and me, an invisible barrier. In many ways, they didn't understand who I was anymore.

I went back to Pittsburgh, Pennsylvania, and the first thing I did was call all my buddies. And these were guys that I went to elementary school with, to high school with, college with. And I'd go down there, and these dudes were still living in the same house, sitting in the same spots on the couch, talking about the same girl problems with the same *Simpsons* posters on the wall and *Family Guy* magnets on the fridge, and I'm thinking, *Jesus Christ! Nothing has changed here at home, but I am a fundamentally different person in every way.* So now I felt like I was disconnected from my friends.

We went out later that night. We were sitting around and drinking beers, and I tried to tell them the stories. So a couple of combat stories, right? And immediately, after about five minutes of telling the story, I found myself sitting alone at the table. And it wasn't anything that they did, but combat can be a buzzkill. It sucks. It's hard. And there's a lot to despair about. You lose people that you love and care about, and you see death and destruction all around you. It's a buzzkill, and we were trying to celebrate. So I get it.

But in that moment, I shut down. I said, "I'm not telling my story to anybody else ever again unless it's a veteran who's been there." And you hear it all the time, like, "These civilians, they just don't get it." So I shut down.

And then my perspective changed when I picked up the new mission of writing *Outlaw Platoon*. I really focused on telling the story of the members of that group. In performing that mission I realized the importance of veterans' storytelling. Because as I wrote that book and told that story, it's like I'm taking the war out of myself and putting it on the page. That was really deeply healing for me. I do fifty public events a year, and it never fails. I go to these events, and there's always somebody in the crowd who comes up to me and says, "You know what? My grandfather was a World War II veteran, but my God! We didn't even know that he served until after he had passed away and we found this dusty box of medals in the garage." Or, "My father was a Vietnam veteran, and he never, ever, ever talked about the war."

I can't help but think back to that moment around my friends. These previous generations of warriors have a similar experience in this day. It's *Screw this. I'm not talking about this anymore*. And it was that dynamic, right there, of veterans shutting down and not telling their story, that I think has caused a great gap between the people that enjoy freedom on a day-to-day basis and the people that protect it. And with each successive generation of warriors, from World War II through today, that gap has gotten wider and wider.

When you join the military, you raise your right hand, you take an oath to protect and defend the people that you love. I look back now; you know why I shut down? I shut down because I took an oath to protect those people, and I realized that my very story of combat was hurting the people that I had taken an oath to protect. Well, I did what all warriors do. I shut down to protect the people that I love and care about.

So storytelling—veterans coming home from the war and telling their stories to civilians who are willing to listen, and listen and be tough; not wince, but listen and be tough, truly listen with a level of respect and understanding—is really the core of what it means to bring our veterans home the right way.

Of course, we're grateful for the VA and the medical treatment that we have there. It's unbelievable. But the problem with veterans coming home is really a cultural issue and less of a clinical one. You've got veterans that come home. It's a veteran's job when they come home from war to educate society about the horrors of war, so that our society then sends leaders to Congress who also know how terrible it is to send people to war and are more careful with the decision when it comes time to do it. It just makes us a better, stronger country when we know what our veterans go through in the pursuit and defense of freedom.

And right now, that is something that is sorely lacking in our country. We've been at war for twenty years. Seriously, we've been at war since 2001. I'm thirty-eight years old. Half of my life, we've been at war. That's all we've known. And yet most of America has no concept of what it means to fight in a war or fight to defend freedom at all. And to me, that's very, very problematic. So that's part of why my mission is trying to do everything I can to bring people, people that enjoy freedom, closer to people that protect it.

I've served with every race and sexual orientation, and all we cared about was the mission first. We came together as brothers and sisters. The American public needs to go back to that. We have more in common than we have differences.

—*Sergeant Mat Best*

★

Not a week goes by that I don't hear from somebody I served with in Iraq, whether it's a text, whether it's an email, whether it's a phone call. So that bond that you get going through these events, you know, something like this, you're tight with these guys forever.

—*Sergeant Major Eric Geressy*

★

My spotter was just as much of a leader as I was, regardless of the title or who organized the missions or any of that. Later, seeing him in other deployments where he was a team leader, I witnessed our passing of the torch. He kept that same mentality that I had with his guys. He was never above or better than anyone. Everyone was on the same level. We were there for the same reason, and we can get this job done together without anyone acting too much like the chief.

—*Sergeant Nick Irving*

★ ★ ★
JOHN WAYNE WALDING

John Wayne Walding in a valley along the Pakistan border where a patrol turned into a BBQ. Intel revealed that the Taliban was going to raid the village. When nothing happened, the patrol bought a goat and had a BBQ to raise morale with their Afghan partners. Afghanistan, 2007.

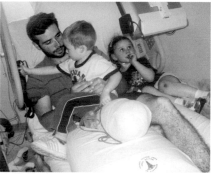

John Wayne recovering in late April 2008 with his son, Sam (age three), and daughter Emma (age four). His children turned three and four while he was hospitalized.

John Wayne competing in a full marathon in 2018.

Family Christmas. *(left to right)* Sam Houston Walding (thirteen), wife Amy, Andie Kate (eight), Hannah Kyle (three), and Emma Grace (fourteen).

All images courtesy of the individual warriors unless otherwise noted.

★ ★ ★
JEREMIAH WORKMAN

Jeremiah Workman and Sgt. Kraft, taken on a rooftop outside of the city of Fallujah circa February 2005.

Jeremiah inspecting one of the displays at the National Museum of the Marine Corps in Triangle, Virginia. *Photo courtesy of the 'Washington Post' via Getty Images*

Jeremiah, along with David Bellavia, speaking at the American Veterans Center conference circa 2009.

★ ★ ★

JOHNNY "JOEY" JONES

After thirty-six hours of intense fighting, Johnny "Joey" Jones rests in an abandoned home his platoon secured during a raid in the Garmsir District of Helmand Province in early June 2010. Ironically, Jones would suffer his injury just a few blocks away from that same location two months later.

Joey sleeping in the ICU at Bethesda Naval Medical Center just days after his injury on August 6, 2010.

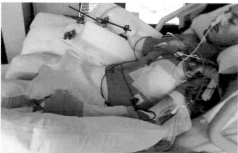

Joey stands onstage with his friend and former boss Zac Brown (of the Zac Brown Band). Joey worked for Brown's for-profit and nonprofit businesses developing the Warrior Week transition program at Brown's Camp Southern Ground.

★ ★ ★
CHAD FLEMING

Chad, his mother, Sylvia, and his father, Jack, circa 1974.

Chad poses proudly in his dress uniform and green beret.

Chad in full battle rattle during his deployment to Afghanistan post-amputation.

Chad (*seated second from left*) backstage during day two of the fourth annual Pepsi's Rock the South Festival, at Heritage Park in Cullman, Alabama—with Blackberry Smoke's Richard Turner, Rock the South lady Sarah Neill, Blackberry Smoke's Brit Turner, RTS lady Taylor Elliott, Colston Galloway, RTS lady Kara Leonard, and former contestant on *Dancing with the Stars* US Army sergeant (ret.) Noah Galloway. *Photo courtesy of Rick Diamond via Getty Images*

1L Fernando Pelayo (*center*), Eagle Company 2nd Squadron, 2nd Styker Cavalry Regiment, during cordon and search in East Rashid Baghdad. September 2007.

HHC Recon Platoon 1–509th Parachute Infantry Regiment, Fort Polk, Louisiana, 1994. SSG Eric Geressy, first row, kneeling on the far right.

Second Platoon Bravo Company, 2nd Battalion, 187th Infantry, 101st Airborne Division Air Assault from Baghdad to Sinjar. May 2003.

General John Kelly USMC SOUTHCOM commander at Eric's retirement ceremony. April 2014.

★ ★ ★
MAT BEST

Mat Best showing his bruised hand as result of a shrapnel wound sustained while breaching a door. Iraq, 2008.

Mat serving as Ranger Team Leader before going out on a Combat Search and Rescue mission. Iraq, 2008

Mat had just assaulted an objective and cleared through a target building. This was a "team selfie" before Mat's unit left. Iraq, 2008.

Mat at home, having fun with his dog "Brehmmy."

★ ★ ★
SCOTT MANN

After retiring from twenty-three years in service, Scott pinned lieutenant bars on his son, Cody, to become an Army infantry officer. 2LT Cody Mann (*left*) and LTC (ret.) Scott Mann. Riverview, Florida, 2020.

Scott volunteering at a Kabul orphanage in January 2010.

Scott performs in a play he wrote about modern war called *Last Out—Elegy of a Green Beret*. It is touring the country and streaming on FOX Nation. According to Mann, telling the story of modern war is one of the most important things we can do to help promote understanding across politics, media, and communities, and is a powerful way for military family members and veterans to heal.

"The people back home don't have any idea what we go through!" says Green Beret Sergeant Danny Patton in the play *Last Out—Elegy of a Green Beret*. LTC (ret.) Scott Mann as Green Beret MSG Danny Pattons during a sold-out performance in New York City, 2019.

DANIEL CRENSHAW

Growing up in Houston, Texas, circa 1993. Dan Crenshaw lost his mom to breast cancer in 1994.

Kandahar Province, Afghanistan, 2012, with SEAL Team 3.

Republican primary ballot position drawing for TX-2. Out of nine ballot positions, Dan's wife, Tara, drew the number-one position. They were pretty happy about that!

★ ★ ★
ADAM KINZINGER

Adam Kinzinger in pilot training in Enid, Oklahoma, 2004. He's preparing for "stand up," where they are quizzed on their airplane knowledge.

(*left to right*) LTC Tim Leverence, MAJ Kinzinger, and MAJ Caleb Ramsey in Lincoln, Nebraska, for the air show in 2016.

Rep. Adam Kinzinger and Sen. John McCain in Rockford, Illinois, at a veteran's event in 2015.

Adam demonstrating his dual roles as a representative and reservist at the US Capitol in 2013.

★ ★ ★
MORGAN LUTTRELL

Morgan Luttrell with his mother and his brother, Marcus.

Morgan's last deployment before retirement. Luttrell and a teammate on a rooftop in Afghanistan.

Morgan and two of his teammates just after an early-morning operation.

Morgan and his brother, Marcus, wearing combat boots to support the Boot Campaign, a nonprofit that supports injured vets.

Sean Parnell with his ranger buddies after his father pinned his Ranger Tab. He went from 225 pounds to 165 pounds in about ninety days.

Sean while on deployment at Forward Operating Base, Bermel, Afghanistan, Paktika Province, circa spring 2007.

Sean patrolling the Hindu Kush mountain range in Afghanistan.

Sean with his children: Emma (*front*), Evan (*middle*), and Ethan (*back left*).

JOHN "JOCKO" WILLINK

★ ★ ★

Jocko Willink engaging in foreign internal defense with a Sri Lankan Special Boat Service commando.

Rooftop command and control position during clearance operations with SEALs, American and Iraqi Soldiers, and US Marines. Ramadi, Iraq, 2006.

Jocko undertaking jungle training in Panama in 1993 as a member of SEAL Team 1, Alpha Platoon.

Jocko speaking on stage at the Extreme Ownership MUSTER in Washington, DC, May 2018. The MUSTER is a two-day premier leadership conference.

CAROLINE JOHNSON

It's always sunny above the clouds. One of Caroline Johnson's favorite parts about flying was getting to enjoy the sunshine up above the layers.

Caroline returned to the Naval Academy to teach leadership and run aviation recruitment. She loved introducing her students to the naval aviation community and encouraging them to chase goals they never knew were even possible.

Families who cheer together stay together. Caroline's brother is also a Naval Academy graduate and Navy pilot. He is married with two kids, and their parents couldn't be prouder to be a Navy family.

★ ★ ★

NICK "THE REAPER" IRVING

Nick and his spotter, Mike Pemberton, soaked in water and blood, entering a safe house after being pinned down by an enemy sniper and ambushed.

Circa 2009, at the end of Nick's deployment. They were finally going home.

A photo of Nick back in his room after an intense night during his record-setting 2009 deployment in Afghanistan.

DAVID BELLAVIA

Staff Sergeant David Bellavia (*second from left*) in Fallujah with Staff Sergeant Colin Fitts (*third from left*).

David throwing the first pitch before Game 3 of the Washington Nationals vs. Los Angeles Dodgers National League Divisional Series in October 2019. *Photo courtesy of Robb Carr/Getty Images Sport via Getty Images*

David giving his acceptance speech at the Hall of Heroes induction ceremony at the Pentagon, June 26, 2019.

★ ★ ★
PETE HEGSETH

Pete with his company, Charlie Company, at the gate between American soil and Cuba, Guantanamo Bay, Cuba, 2004.

Pete on a dismounted security patrol as a platoon leader at Guantanamo Bay.

Pete with two of his unit leadership at their reunion after their Iraq deployment in 2007.

PART IV

LEADERSHIP IN LIFE

I want to be judged by what my subordinates do, I want to be judged by what kind of people they are when they come home, and I want to be judged by what they were able to do because of me, after me.

—*Staff Sergeant David Bellavia*

★

The military really helped me learn how strong I am and what truly is possible. It really taught me that it doesn't matter where you come from—it doesn't matter, any of this stuff. You can achieve it if you put your mind to it.

—*Lieutenant Commander Caroline Johnson*

CHAPTER 12

LIEUTENANT COMMANDER

JOHN "JOCKO" WILLINK

UNITED STATES NAVY

I 100 percent believe that

going into combat made

me a better person.

It was probably ten or eleven o'clock at night; I forget what time exactly. We were setting up Marc Lee's angel flight. In the summer of 2006, we had been in Ramadi about three months, taking part in sustained combat operations that eventually became known as the Second Battle of Ramadi. My task unit had been doing extremely dangerous operations, taking out a bunch of bad guys. We had developed an air of invincibility, not just within our team, but with our army and marine corps brothers—an incredible brotherhood had formed on the battlefield with these soldiers, sailors, airmen, and marines. They would see us go out, learn that we'd eliminated a bunch of enemy soldiers, and we'd always come back. All of us would come back.

When Marc got killed it was a shock to everyone's soul. Marc had a larger-than-life personality, always smiling, always gregarious. He was such a brave and incredible guy. He was certainly at the top of everyone's list in thinking that nothing could ever happen to this guy. He was just too strong of a human. To have him be the first SEAL team member killed in Iraq was a crushing blow. Not just to my task unit, but to everyone on the ground.

So that night, we were at the morgue getting ready for Marc's last flight home. We had to escort Marc down a small, dirty road that led from the morgue to the airfield at Camp Ramadi. The atmosphere was silent. Solemn and respectful. Our minds were on the job at hand. So when we stepped outside from the morgue, we were a little overwhelmed to see hundreds of people had assembled along that route. They were all silent, and as Marc passed, each individual soldier, sailor, airman, or marine stood at attention and saluted.

He was loaded into the helicopter. We all stood there, watching as the helicopter flew off into the darkness.

★★

Lieutenant Commander Jocko Willink served in the United States Navy with distinction for twenty years. He enlisted in 1990, and shortly after completing basic training, he attended BUD/S as a member of class 177 in Coronado, California. Upon completion of BUD/S he reported to SEAL Team 1, where he spent seven years as an enlisted SEAL operator before being selected to attend Officer Candidate School. Upon graduation, Jocko reported back to the SEAL teams, where he spent the rest of his career.

During the Iraq War, he deployed as a SEAL platoon commander on SEAL Team 7 and then led SEAL Team 3's Task Unit Bruiser, which undertook operations during the Second Battle of Ramadi. They worked in support of the "Ready First" Brigade of the US Army's 1st Armored Division. Task Unit Bruiser unleashed devastation on enemy fighters, aggressively taking the fight to the enemy and killing scores of insurgents. The valor and effectiveness of Task Unit Bruiser was evident by their impact on the battlefield. They ultimately became the most highly decorated Special Operations unit of the Iraq War.

Jocko is the recipient of the Silver Star, the Bronze Star for combat valor, and many other individual and unit awards.

Jocko went on to serve as the officer in charge of Naval Special Warfare Group 1 Training Detachment. While there, he designed, developed, and oversaw the training of all West Coast SEAL teams. With his training, SEAL platoons and troops were prepared for harsh and violent combat deployments. He formally developed leadership curriculum for the SEALs.

The discipline instilled in him during his Navy Seal career extended beyond the battlefield and his military career. He earned a black belt in Brazilian jiujitsu and has helped coach a number of mixed martial arts combatants.

After leaving the navy in 2010, Jocko worked with fellow SEAL team member Leif Babin to create the highly successful and influential leadership consulting service Echelon Front. The two also collaborated on the *New York Times* bestsellers *Extreme Ownership: How U.S. Navy SEALs Lead and Win* and *The Dichotomy of Leadership*. Jocko has also written the *New York Times* bestsellers *Discipline Equals Freedom: Field Manual* and *Leadership Strategy and Tactics* and the bestselling children's books *Way of the Warrior Kid*, *Marc's Mission*, *Where There's a Will*, and *Mikey and the Dragons*. Jocko also anchors his top-rated podcast, *Jocko Podcast*, which talks about leadership and human nature through the lens of war and human struggle.

An acknowledged leader and winner, Jocko came from humble beginnings. He grew up on a dirt road in a small town in New England. He loved the ocean and being in the water, and for as long as he can remember, he knew he wanted to serve in the military. As a kid, he wore old surplus camouflage uniforms and would run through the woods at night with his friends. They burned wine corks to create face paint for camouflage. For an assignment in elementary school, when asked what Jocko wanted to be as an adult, he wrote "marine or soldier." According to him, "I am the luckiest guy in the world because I got to do exactly what I was put here to do. One thing about the SEAL teams is that it was never work for me. I never considered being in the SEAL teams work. I wasn't the only one who felt that way. I had a job for twenty years, but I never went to work one day. Shooting machine guns. Blowing things up. Diving. Parachuting. One school I went to, they taught us how to break into cars and steal them and then drive them away. Not just drive them, but race them. It's totally ridiculous. The best job ever."

★★

Being there, seeing Marc off like that, was simultaneously the most humbling and proud experience I have ever had. I stood there thinking, *Here I am, standing next to a fallen hero, standing next to a guy that just gave his life for his friends, a man that gave his life for us.* It is very humbling to stand next to a hero like that. And at the same time, we were—everyone there in that line—we were all willing to make that sacrifice. And to know that I was a part of something that powerful is something I will forever be proud of and that will stay with me for the rest of my life. It is something I will never forget.

THE RIGHT THING, THE HARD THING

I enlisted in the navy because I wanted to be a SEAL. I had heard about the SEAL teams, but I actually didn't know a lot about them. In the 1980s there were no movies about the SEALs. I didn't know of any books about them. I watched all kinds of war movies as a kid—*Platoon, Full Metal Jacket, Apocalypse Now.* There was a lot of mystique out there about the SEALs but not a lot of information. I heard that they did the hardest training and the guys would go into combat. That's what I wanted.

When I joined the navy, I told my dad. He asked what I was going to do. I told him I was going to try to become a SEAL. He said, "I don't think you're going to like the navy." When I asked him why he said something like "Because you don't like listening to other people and you don't like authority, so you're going to hate the military." Both my parents were schoolteachers, and there was some truth to what he was saying. I wasn't a great student. I wasn't a great athlete. I was not focused on these things. I got into some trouble at school and around town.

I was also a young kid, naïve about the military. I looked at my dad and said, "No, Dad, it's the SEAL teams. It's a team. You don't have to follow orders." I didn't know that being part of a team meant sometimes you do follow orders. And that is a good thing.

The navy turned out to be a great fit for me. When I got there, I was a blank slate. I knew I wanted to be a SEAL, but I didn't know exactly what it would take to get there. Luckily, the navy spelled out what I needed to do to be successful. You have to fold your T-shirt a certain way, you've got to make your bed a certain way. I realized, *Hey, I can do these things that they're telling me to do and I can do them well, and that will help me progress.*

Looking back on it now, in high school, I had a rebellious streak. I was a bit of a troublemaker. But I worked hard at things I liked. I had a hard-core attitude. When I was on the soccer team, I got in trouble for singing military chants and cadences while we were on the field. I focused my energy on the wrong things, sometimes. If I got in a fight, it was usually because I saw someone taking advantage of another kid's weakness and I wanted to stand up to that.

Now I can see that that was a part of my warrior mentality. A warrior is someone that does what they're supposed to do. A warrior is someone that is supposed to protect people who can't protect themselves. A warrior is someone that does the right thing, even when it's the hard thing to do. Warriors are ready to engage, to make things happen.

THE BEST AND THE WORST OF US

One of the realities of being a warrior is combat. Like other modern warriors, Jocko relished the opportunity to put his training and skills to use in defending this country and those others who needed the protection our military provides for them.

Combat was the best experience in my life and, obviously, it was also the worst experience of my life. Being able to lead troops in combat and having all that responsibility was an absolute honor. Every day that I was overseas, each one of those days . . . those are the best days that I had in my life. And then, of course, those days when I had guys get wounded or killed are the worst days of my life. There are these dichotomies in combat. It produced the best memories that I have and the absolute worst memories that I have. Combat reveals the best part of humanity and also shows aspects of unmitigated evil. You come to understand that humanity has a dark side that needs to be confronted and dealt with.

Combat is horrible and it's awful and it's a nightmare; but it's also the best thing, too. So how do I reconcile these two thoughts being in my head? One way that I can explain it is like this: if you've ever known someone that had cancer and who survived, think of their mentality. Often when you talk to that person, they say, "It's the best thing that's happened to me. I wouldn't wish it on anyone, but I learned so much about myself. I learned to appreciate things. I learned to see other perspectives. It was humbling to not be in control." So people learn so much from having cancer. And that's the way I feel about combat as well. I wouldn't wish it on someone, but I'm absolutely glad that I had those experiences that shaped me as a person.

Combat gives you a better perspective of the world. It gives you a better understanding of the preciousness of human life, the fragility of human life. It makes you better understand what you should be appreciative of. It makes you understand your limitations. It absolutely humbles you because there are things that are beyond your control, and you need to learn to understand those things and accept things that you can't control. And you have to learn to take control of the things that are under your control.

So much stigma surrounds going to war. Some people believe that it warps your mentality or that it changes you in a negative way. People think that when someone goes to war, that person comes home from war broken. And I just don't believe that was true for me, and I don't think that is true for a lot of us that served in combat. I understand that it has a different impact on different people, but I 100 percent think that going to combat made me a better person.

THE RESPONSIBILITY OF LEADERSHIP AND THE REALITY OF LOSS

Just as combat can be both the best and worst thing, leadership can be a dual-edged sword. It took a while for me to make a connection and apply a lesson for myself that I'd pass along to others.

When people are feeling afraid, that's okay. It's perfectly fine. What causes a problem is when people don't understand what the source of those feelings is. They don't understand why they feel sick. They don't understand why they feel nervous. They don't understand what that is, and that actually puts them in a downward spiral. They don't understand what they're feeling, and that lack of awareness makes them nervous about what they're feeling, which is even worse. Then they feel even more nervous, which makes them even more scared, and it just turns into a downward spiral.

If you understand fear, then you understand what is happening when you think to yourself, *Oh, I feel sick right now*, or *My stomach feels queasy*, or *I'm sweating*, or *I'm preoccupied*. You know those feelings are rooted in fear, and that's perfectly fine. Just accept that. That's part of your body preparing to go into combat, so it's totally normal. And that's something I always felt was important to pass on to the younger guys. Otherwise, they'd be thinking, *Why do I feel this way? Am I a coward? Am I horrified? Am I not going to perform well?*

The reality is that it's perfectly fine. You'll get used to it, and it's no factor.

Another element of fear is how you deal with it over a sustained period of time. And the answer is you have to get to a point where you accept the fact that you can die. You have to accept death. Once I accepted death, I wasn't afraid of anything happening to me.

But the thing that I was always afraid of, the thing that did make me feel sick, the thing that would make me feel uncomfortable every single day, was not me getting wounded or me getting killed. It was one of my guys getting wounded or killed. That's the fear that I dealt with. The fear of your friends getting wounded or killed was the hardest thing.

I didn't realize how heavily that weighed on me until I got home from my last deployment. I was home for about a month, and I was on my post-deployment leave, so we had wrapped everything up. A week into that leave, I woke up one day. I just felt like a weight had lifted off my shoulders. I just felt good. I just felt relieved about something, and it felt really good.

I was sitting there thinking, *Why do I feel so good right now?* And then it hit me. The reason I felt good was because I wasn't distraught and agonizing over the fact that one of my guys might get wounded or killed. It was one of those things that while I was on deployment, I felt it, but I didn't consciously think about it. It was a subconscious grinding on my soul—I didn't realize how heavily it weighed on me until I got home and enough time went by that it allowed that weight to be lifted. And then I realized, man, that was the only thing on my mind during deployment. All day, all night, there is only one thought: *Are all my guys going to come back off this operation today?*

And when we lost Marc, that weight was on me. With Marc being the first SEAL team member killed in Iraq, I had no formal training as a leader how to deal with the loss of a team member.

There was no handbook to follow. We just didn't have the experience with death at that time in the SEAL teams to understand what it does to guys and how we need to handle it. I was the task unit commander, so obviously, I had to figure it out. I had to figure it out, not only for myself, but more important, for the guys. And Marc was our friend. He was our friend that was killed. Gone. Just like that. It was awful. But the war doesn't stop, and there are still mujahedeen fighters that are out there, and we need to go back and continue to do our job.

So even if there was no training in how to deal with loss, I applied the same rules that we did to any combat situation. You need to assess what's happening; you need to figure out how to respond to it; you need to start taking action, move in that direction, and then keep an open mind and play off of the feedback that you get.

So that's what I did. Don't get me wrong, of course; we had a protocol to follow in terms of the official procedures that we went through—the notification of the family, the paperwork that has to be filled out. But the other side, the emotional side, the human side, I had to figure that out and improvise and adapt as we went along.

I looked at it like this: *Okay, I know the guys are going to need to stand down. We're going to need to take a day or two off to say goodbye to Marc and get him flown out of there. The next day, we've got to do some kind of memorial service.* And then my instinct was, *What we need to do is we need to go back to work.* And it wasn't just an instinct of what will be good for the task unit, but it's also what we needed to do as SEALs, as frogmen, and as American fighting men. This is what we do. There are still missions that have to be accomplished. The army and the marine corps have lost many, many men, and they are still losing them. The war doesn't stop. And I also thought that the worst thing we could do is wait around and not do anything. I didn't want us to drown in our sorrows. We needed to get back in the fight, and that's exactly what Marc would have wanted us to do as well. He would have wanted us to get back in the fight.

So we took a day off; we stood down to see Marc off—to send him on his last flight home. The next day we started planning, and then we got our gear back on, locked and loaded our weapons, and went back out and took the fight to the enemy and did our job. We did our duty. We did exactly what Marc would have wanted us to do.

In his role as a leadership consultant—and using the SEAL teams as a model—Jocko has learned to dispel one persistent misconception: that a rigid top-down hierarchy of command exists in the military. The belief is that leaders issue orders and others blindly follow. Of course, during his career, Jocko saw examples of that style of leadership, leadership by fear and intimidation, but he also saw how ineffective it proved to be.

The last thing in the world I would want is my guys to be afraid of me or think that I don't know how to control my temper. If they're afraid of me, they're not going to tell me when they don't agree with me. If they're afraid of me, they're not going to tell me when they think I've got the wrong plan. If they're afraid of me, they're not going to come to me and tell me when they need a break.

The fact is, fear can be used to intimidate people and get people to do what you want them to do. That may work in the short term. And, unfortunately, some leaders get the idea reinforced in their minds that losing your temper is a good thing because it makes what you want to have happen, happen. But it doesn't help you build a relationship. It doesn't help build a team. It doesn't help people trust you. People aren't going to be there for you when you need them to be there. They're not going to give you any resistance.

And as a leader, I never wanted people working for me that gave me no resistance. I want people that are going to actually push back if they don't agree with me, or they're going to offer their suggestions on how to do something.

I saw it over and over again inside the military, and I see it in my consulting business now. Yes, you can gain some short-term results by being a tyrant that yells and screams at people. But in terms of the long-term unification of a team, it is not going to be there, and that's just the way it is.

The leader that had the biggest impression on me inside the SEAL teams was a guy I wrote about in my book, *Leadership Strategy and Tactics*. In that book I call him Delta Charlie, and he was an extremely experienced SEAL officer. He had combat experience from the invasion of Grenada when almost no one in the SEAL teams had combat experience. He had come up through the ranks to become a senior enlisted noncommissioned officer, and then got his commission and became an officer. He had a legendary status inside the SEAL teams. We all knew his reputation. He was respected by everyone. But even with all that experience and all that legendary status and all that knowledge and all that skill, he still was the most humble guy in our SEAL platoon, and he was our platoon commander. He was our leader—the highest-ranking guy in our platoon, but he was a guy that would take out the trash every night. He was a guy that would, when it came time to plan a training operation, say, "Hey, Jocko, why don't you come up with a plan for this?" even though I was one of the youngest guys in the platoon. So those types of leaders, those humble leaders, those were always the best leaders that I had.

I also believe in leading yourself. I feel fortunate that, unlike some veterans, my transition to civilian life was smooth.

I found a new mission and I started executing on my new mission, and that became my focus. I tell veterans all the time, when you get out of the military, you need to find a new mission. And that mission can be whatever you choose. Maybe your mission is that you are going to be the best dad or that mission is going to do triathlons, or "I'm going to get good at this sport," or "I'm going to start a new company," or "I'm going to be a great employee somewhere." It doesn't really matter what you choose as your new mission, you need to find a new mission.

Because when you're in the military, you've got this incredible job, you've got the most meaningful mission a human being can ever have, which is to protect freedom and democracy in the world, and you're working with a bunch of people who all share that common mission, that common goal. And in the SEAL teams, these people are not only your coworkers, they are your best friends. And you have memories and friendships—friendships forged in the fire of war—and you have shared experiences and a common language and a common history. It is family. In many ways, even closer than family. And then one day, your time is up. You retire. You get out. Your time is up, and you leave. And all those things, in one day, are gone. And if you lag around and don't find a new mission, you're going to drift, and eventually, the drift will lean toward the path of least resistance, and the path of least resistance leads down. And you don't want to get on that path. You want to find a new mission, and you want to go and start to try to execute on that new mission. Just because you finished with your service to the country doesn't mean you don't have anything left to give. Not even close. Take what you learned. Take what you know. Take the discipline you have. Take the knowledge and experience you earned and put them to use in the world. You learned to lead in the military—and it is not just the military that needs leaders. The entire world needs leaders. Go out there, find a new mission, and *lead*.

CHAPTER 13

LIEUTENANT COMMANDER
CAROLINE JOHNSON
UNITED STATES NAVY

We were always being told these Iraqi cities were under imminent attack. ISIS was going to overrun one or another in twenty-four or forty-eight hours. It was nine years, one month, and ten days from the time I started at the Naval Academy to when I was able to do my job in combat. And that's a lot of education and training. And so here I am overhead, and I'm trained to protect these innocent people. And all it would have taken for us would be to push in, drop a bomb, and neutralize these bad guys in the vicinity of civilians. That's what we trained for, but we weren't being given permission to do it.

As I hurtled along at five hundred miles an hour plus, my view of the black-and-white screen remained fairly clear. My aching backside and back pain faded into the background as I forgot many days in the air and zoomed in on the enemy. The muzzle flash from the tanks was clear. At first the target wasn't. This was 2014, and the mainstream media had finally begun to share with the world what we already knew. ISIS was committing horrendous acts of violence in Iraq. In particular, on this mission, we were in northwest Iraq, flying in the vicinity of Mount Sinjar.

Our intelligence on the boat had briefed us on the threat ISIS posed to the Yazidis, a religious and ethnic minority in Iraq, and how thousands of the innocent had fled to Mount Sinjar, their homeland.

I shifted my focus from the black-and-white screen to the glass canopy outside to see an unfiltered view of what was unfolding on the ground. My pulse quickened as fiery explosions erupted in a village that clung to the north side of the mountain. My aircraft was low on fuel so my pilot and I had to head to the tanker.

As we departed the close air support (CAS) stack, I thought about the situation below. We didn't just have those two armored personnel carriers to worry about. ISIS fighters also had an up-armored Humvee on site. The fighters were lobbing grenades at the Yazidi village and the men, women, and children were running for their lives. Like an impatient customer at a gas station, we soared along taking on fuel as fast as we could. As my pilot focused on refueling, I was tracking on the back radio the struggle between ISIS and the civilians, growing more and more impatient. Not unlike my mom friends at home—dealing with young kids in the heat of summer, worrying about the ice cream cones melting all over the back of the family SUV—I too was stressed about a situation I couldn't control.

Only I was a highly trained, highly skilled weapon systems officer (WSO, pronounced "wizzo") sitting in the back seat of an $80 million aircraft itching to do my job to defend the defenseless. As the minutes ticked by, all I could think of were the Yazidi people, and the terror they were experiencing at the hands of an inhumane and relentless persecutor.

A few minutes later, we flew over Mount Sinjar again and my sensors locked onto the action below. A thrill ran through me. There they were! We got a lock on the three vehicles and followed them as they drove along the highway. I reported my status to the Spec Ops JTAC, who was working to coordinate the air strike we hoped to deliver. For the moment, though, we were all stuck in a holding pattern. We couldn't do a thing, they couldn't do a thing, until everything was run up the chain of command and we were granted permission to use lethal force. We'd been flying operations in Iraq for the past fifty-five days, but we had only gone kinetic, or been authorized the use of lethal force, for one day at that point.

Finally, and from who knows where and from who knows whom, the decision came down. I heard the words I'd been waiting for: "Hellcat 26, cleared hot!"

Hell yes. It was game time! This was why we were out here. This was why I'd put up with the inane rules at the Academy. This was why I'd sucked it up when I was passed over to become a pilot. This was why I'd driven myself so hard for so long. We were about to deliver two laser-guided JDAM with 480 pounds of TNT packed into each supersmart weapon. As a weapon systems officer, a naval flight officer, and one of the very few women in the sky, I was happy to be doing my job, supporting our troops on the ground, defending the Yazidi people, and taking it to ISIS.

★★

Caroline Johnson was born in Colorado Springs, Colorado. Despite the fact that it is a military town—Peterson Air Force Base, Cheyenne Mountain Complex, the United States Air Force Academy, and the United States Army's Fort Carson are all within easy proximity to the city—Caroline grew up pretty distanced and not knowing much about the military. Sure, her family sponsored air force cadets and would attend graduation ceremonies at the Academy. That was a part of being a patriotic American. But she didn't know the military was a career possibility for her.

Colorado was a wonderful place to grow up with her family. She and her older brother, Craig, took full advantage of all the outdoor activities that the area had to offer. Her parents met while living in Aspen, and skiing was a large part of all their lives. Besides her parents, another family member figured prominently in Caroline's life—her paternal grandmother, aka Grammy, who served overseas in World War II as a civilian nurse and also worked in that capacity as a part of the Manhattan Project in Hanford, Washington, and at Los Alamos, New Mexico.

Grammy was the matriarch of the family and an independent soul. She lived to be a hundred, and is remembered as a fiercely strong, fun, and adventurous woman. She was a huge role model for Caroline, and in pictures of the two of them, the resemblance is uncanny.

Grammy's husband, Chester Johnson, was a navy lieutenant and ophthalmologist who performed medical research during the Bikini Atoll hydrogen bomb testing. Her maternal grandfather, Jay Gaulden, served his country as a glider pilot in the Army Air Corps in World War II, crash-landing behind enemy lines before making his way back. He survived the war but died of polio three days before the birth of Caroline's mother, Nancy.

Despite this familial history of service, Caroline remained unaware of what her grandparents had done. Like many of the Greatest Generation, they came back to America and quietly went about the business of creating a better life for future members of the family, the community, and the nation. Her family made their living as doctors, lawyers, and businesspeople; growing up, Caroline and her brother didn't fully understand what career military life meant and what an honor it was to serve.

An outstanding student and athlete—Caroline took advantage of the United States Olympic training facilities and coaches in Colorado Springs—she also participated in Girl Scouts, was a National Honor Society scholar, and a debutante. The most formative experience for her was studying abroad in Germany as part of the Congress-Bundestag Youth Exchange program. She was sponsored by the United States Congress to serve as a youth ambassador there.

Some of Caroline's German friends had experienced the Berlin Wall coming down and talked about the pivotal role America played in that historic event. Learning the role the US military played in global issues and international relationships at a young age drove Caroline to want to impact the world for the better. It was her time abroad that solidified her decision to make a difference.

Returning from her year abroad, Caroline applied for schools to pursue her undergraduate degree at, with an eye on eventually becoming a doctor. Her brother had been selected to attend the Naval Academy and, on a visit there, Caroline fell in love with the campus and the tradition. Her sights changed, and she received her Academy appointment in 2005.

Originally attracted to the travel opportunities, Caroline entered the Academy wanting to be a ship driver, a surface warfare officer in navy speak. Eventually, though, she opted to pursue aviation. Her brother had made the same choice; her father was a civilian pilot, and her grandfather had flown gliders. "When my brother and I both ended up flying my mother told us both how proud her dad would have been to know that we'd continued in the family aviation tradition."

No doubt he would have been even more so after Caroline became a weapon systems officer flying in the navy's F/A-18 aircraft. She finished at the top of her flight school class, earning the Paul F. Lawrence Award as the number one strike fighter graduate. Eventually she flew forty-two combat missions against ISIS and Taliban forces in Iraq, Syria, and Afghanistan, accruing more than nine hundred flight hours in the F/A-18F, also known as the Super Hornet. She was proud to serve as a member of VFA-213, the world-famous Fighting Blacklions, eventually earning her instructor and combat mission commander designations.

Later she earned her master's degree and returned to the Naval Academy as a senior leadership instructor and program manager. She recounted her experiences in the 2019 book *Jet Girl: My Life in War, Peace, and the Cockpit of the Navy's Most Lethal Aircraft, the F/A-18 Super Hornet*. Today she travels the country as a professional speaker, appearing at businesses, schools, universities, and conferences.

★★

What was so special about the moments that led to our attack that took out sixteen enemy fighters was that this was a case of being in the right place at the right time in the right aircraft with the right people all doing the right thing. That's what makes for a righteous kill, right?

From the men and women on the ground coordinating efforts, to the drone relaying comms, to us being a two-seat fighter with a pilot and a weapons officer coordinating our efforts, to the professionals who had gathered the intelligence, we were all on point. The two JDAM penetrated the lead vehicle and flipped the second one. We were cleared an immediate reattack, which was not an easy thing to do. I selected the laser-guided Maverick missile, targeted the weapon, and within seconds we neutralized the remaining Humvee. We had to get visual evidence of the kills, and the scene was littered with dead bodies. Not something easy to see or to forget, but neither was the sight of all those civilians, all those Yazidi, being massacred.

That deployment I flew a total of forty-two combat flights. We were awarded a bunch of medals and unit citations. And it wasn't just the Blacklions. There were eight other squadrons aboard the boat. Each of which was equally active. Yes, we were first to drop bombs on ISIS in Iraq and Syria, but the fight went on after we left.

"Good hits! Good hits!" continued to be heard over the comms. On good nights, I can still hear those words.

ACADEMY DAZE

My parents always said, "You do you." That meant that I was encouraged and supported to be my authentic self. That sometimes came into conflict with what I was being told at the Naval Academy. Inane rules and being controlled were always very difficult for me. As a kid, I was a tomboy, and I grew up pretty rough-and-tumble. Except around Grammy, who made sure I brushed my hair and was prim and proper.

During high school, I evolved to be pretty feminine, but I never lost my tomboy roots. When I went to the Naval Academy, that all changed. There was a huge value placed on masculinity, even for women, and the uniforms and grooming regulations made it so that many women felt like they had to look like mini men. For the first time I rebelled. I didn't like the idea of being told to look like a guy. Subconsciously my brain said, *I'm going to be full girl.* I memorized all the uniform regulations and would then go out to get my nails done to the exact specification. That wasn't something I did with any regularity before, but I did it religiously beginning at the Academy. We also had a curfew regulation—lights out and in bed by 11 p.m. I'd stay up with my flashlight, studying. We weren't allowed to nap during the day, but I did. Silly things like that, but I had to assert my independence somehow.

When I started at the Academy, my class had about 1,200 midshipmen and we were 14 percent women. That wasn't surprising to me, but I didn't think it mattered. I walked into the Naval Academy and thought I was on level ground. I had earned my spot there. I could do all the athletic tests, and I knew I could handle the academic rigor. My best subjects were math and science, so that was no issue for me. But it was for some people. The Naval Academy is where I first learned I was a minority and where I experienced different expectations and treatment because I didn't look like the majority.

I took every advanced, honors, or AP class I could in high school. Our high school had an engineering program, and it was the first one west of the Mississippi. It was a big deal to have this engineering program. In my freshman year, I was good at math and science, so I said, "Of course I'm going to join the engineering program." Our first semester-long assignment was a research paper, about what engineering major we envisioned having and what our career path would be.

And I raised my hand—of course, there were only two girls in the class, me and Holly. And I said, "Well, Mr. So-and-so, what if we don't want to study engineering?" And he said with a chuckle, "What do you want to do? Make Barbie dolls?"

I said, "No, actually, I want to be a doctor, but I'm in this engineering class because it's the best program this side of the Mississippi." And he scoffed, "Yeah, yeah, sure, little girl." I wrote my paper about engineering Barbie dolls, specifically about being a mechanical engineer who designs the machinery and process that goes into making a Barbie doll. Just to prove a point. I got an A plus.

Though it was just a snide remark by a teacher, it was small stuff like that and the way that I was treated in that class that I withdrew out of the engineering program. I said, "I don't need these haters. I don't need to be treated that way." And it really drove me away from engineering. Otherwise, at the Naval Academy, I would have majored in engineering or another STEM major. Instead, I majored in economics.

At the Academy, I adopted this girly-girl façade to survive. It was easier to go along with other people's perception of me than work to conform to a system where I would always stand out. . . . I was tall. I was blonde. I was gregarious and bubbly. People assumed I was ditsy and privileged, so I played along. People made a lot of assumptions. I would go across the dorms to visit my brother—he was two years ahead of me—at his room. I needed and wanted his advice. He was my big brother, right? Eventually he told me that I should stop coming around his room. I couldn't understand why, so he told me that people were talking about me and about him. They thought we were dating, and it wasn't good for him because I was a plebe, I was a freshman.

And I think what people don't realize is that over time, it's those small events in life that build up; they become a mountain that seems insurmountable. And who wants to climb a mountain if they can't summit? If people don't feel like the goal is achievable or they can really succeed in a career, they're going to turn away. So it doesn't seem like it was a big deal back then, but even those small things kind of built up. And I didn't realize it then. I just chose a different direction and said, *Hey, I'm going to be the best at something else*. In hindsight, I see that I maybe I shouldn't have had to course correct like that.

Now that's one of the reasons I'm a huge advocate for young women and young men. I tell them, "You can do anything, it doesn't matter what the rest of the world thinks." I encourage them to dream big: "You want to do that? Absolutely. You do it." If solicited, I add my advice. "Here's the best way to achieve that goal and the things I know that can get you there, but let me connect you with somebody else who has been there and can help you."

FLIGHT DREAMS AND NIGHTMARES

When it came time to choose a career path in the navy, Caroline chose aviation. As a kid in Colorado Springs, she had seen the Blue Angels and the Thunderbirds, the navy and air force's flight demonstration squadrons, flying overhead. But it wasn't until she went to the Naval Academy and met real-life aviators that she realized flying was a possibility for her. From then on, the sky was wide open.

I only wanted to be a pilot. Front seat. I had all the qualifications. When selections went out I was made a naval flight officer, an NFO, a back-seater. I was heartbroken. I shared that with my brother, who was in pilot training, and he convinced me that NFO was the best-kept secret in the navy. All the perks without all the stress is what he told me. I said okay, but I still wanted to be a pilot. By the time I got down to Pensacola, I had gotten my private pilot's license. I knew that if you finished number one or number two in your initial navy training and you had all the physical qualifications, they would let you transition from NFO to pilot.

I finished at the top of my class, but I wasn't able to switch to the front-seat training. The navy had too many pilots at that point. They were letting student pilots go, releasing them from active duty if they wanted out with no obligation to pay back their college tuition.

So much for becoming a pilot, but I eventually learned that as a WSO, an NFO flying in fighter jets, I could play a vital role. It wasn't the role I had initially hoped for, but it was a challenging and necessary role. Going through training, I controlled as many of the factors as I could to get to my new goal. I got 100 percent scores on my exams. I did well in my flight training. I eventually achieved my new goal of flying in Super Hornets and through it all learned that sometimes circumstances are out of your control. That was hard to accept, but I made the best of it.

I also had to learn to accept that what we were doing was inherently dangerous.

When you're the age I was, because you have so much training, because you're so confident because of all the repetitions you do, you're prepared, prepared, prepared. That goes for takeoff and landing on aircraft carriers as well as employing live ordnance on the enemy. As a result, you develop a larger-than-life attitude. You feel untouchable. Regardless of the situation, you say to yourself, "All right, I've got this." And when you stare death in the face a couple of times on a carrier landing, or you have a couple of near misses with weapons being fired at you, you learn what that feels like. You learn what it is like to truly have your life flash in front of you. Until then, you really don't know what fear is like.

You gain a healthy appreciation for what you do; you realize why your mom worries about you. And you don't tell her about those near misses until years later. Then you start losing friends, and they are not just names in the news but people you know. It's your classmate, squadron mate, or best friend, and you're sitting there watching TV and the ticker goes across the bottom of the screen and you realize that's Val. That airplane going down in Kyrgyzstan, that was Tyler Voss. In your mind, you see what their last seconds were like, because you were in that same spot a week before and it was only by the skin of your teeth that you pulled it out and for some reason they did not.

It was really hard for me being in the back seat. I didn't have control of the aircraft. And landing on an aircraft carrier, you're just petrified every single time. Your legs shake. You have to trust your pilot, and for a type A or even OCD-type person, it's tough to put your life in somebody else's hands. But then you realize how talented and well trained they are.

Still, stuff happens. We were coming in to land one night late after a combat mission, and all of a sudden the whole plane fell out from under us. Literally, we just went plummeting. Like you see those rides at the amusement park where it's like the fall to death. Our plane started doing that. My pilot immediately added max power, but there was a delay in spin-up. And microseconds are life in that environment. We heard the screaming over the radio: "Wave off! Wave off! Power, power, power!" And I saw a sea of flashing red lights. And it's just—that's what death almost looks like.

In an instant we slammed down, four feet from the end of the flight deck. The entire jet, a 44,000-pound aircraft, hopped like a dime-store bouncy ball down the runway until we had a fly-in engagement, and then the whole plane stopped, came to a screeching halt, which is pretty petrifying. My pilot didn't fly for over a week after that. They put him on suicide watch.

And I got up and I flew the next day. And that day's pilot said,

"Are you sure you're okay to fly?" And I was like, "Yeah, I'm fine. I'm good to go," and he's like, "Do you know where you hit last night?" And I said, "It was a close call, freak accident, no big deal. Those things happen." So he walked me up before our flight, and he said, "Look, this is where you hit," and showed me our hook impact point, four feet from the end of the runway. Most landings don't leave a distinct hook impact point; often they scrape a small line in the nonskid where the jet glides in. If it's a hard impact, the hook can chip away the nonskid down to the steel of the flight deck. So literally, from where we stood at that hook impact point, you had to look another hundred feet down the runway until you saw another. And that was pretty sobering, to realize how close we were. My pilot was one of the landing signal officers out on the flight deck the night before. He was responsible for keeping planes safe and talking the pilots down to land, and he had been one of the guys screaming over the radio at us.

A lot of times when we were out there providing overwatch on the ground forces, we worked with the SEAL teams. When they were out there outside the wire, our job was to alert them to groups of ISIS coming at them. Sometimes we'd be talking to a SEAL on the radio; other times it would be an aviator who was embedded with the team. When we headed home after flying our mission, whoever was on the radio would tell us to have a safe landing. "No, no, no," I'd tell them, "You guys be safe on the ground." And some of them would reply, "No. No. No. I'd rather be getting shot at than trying to land on that aircraft carrier out there in the middle of the dark ocean." So it was kind of strange to think that a SEAL was thinking that what we were doing was dangerous. The irony.

It wasn't the only irony, though. As a WSO my primary job was managing the tactical comms and coordination of our jet. That meant I was the one who would check in with the guys on the ground. Hearing a female voice triggered something in them, I guess. I was warned about this by an instructor, but I was still surprised when one time I heard feedback on my radio. I was hearing my own voice coming back at me with a delay, like when you have a bad cellphone signal. It was then that I realized that the ground troops were playing my voice over the loudspeaker on their up-armored Suburban.

Part of our job, and part of the job of the guys on the ground, was to intimidate the enemy. So the point of them playing my voice loud enough so everyone could hear was to let the enemy know that even though their women couldn't even drive cars, we had an American woman flying overhead who could, if you mess with us, drop bombs on you. The guys in the cockpit—I always flew with males—were puzzled when they heard that interference. They'd laugh, and I'd tell them that maybe that was the first time for them hearing that, but I got it all the time.

ANOTHER MISSION—TRANSITION

Coming home is difficult. For veterans, returning from war means something different for each individual, and over the past two decades of the war on terrorism we've learned to tread delicately when addressing combat experiences. Applying those lessons to this pandemic is going to be important to help people "come home" and successfully navigate their way back to a new normal. Society writ large can learn some lessons from the veteran community on how to process their experiences and to name the things we've lived through. I've done a lot of work on moral injury. I participated in a think tank in Washington, DC, called the Coming Home Dialogues. It's sponsored by the National Endowment for the Humanities, and it utilizes literature to look at the process of returning from combat and introducing veterans to the concepts of moral injury and post-traumatic stress. And moral injury is what it sounds like. An injury to your core beliefs, experiencing something that challenges your sense of right and wrong, or executing an order to achieve mission success that might have violated your own morality. And that doesn't always mean what you did, but sometimes what you weren't allowed to do.

When we reentered Iraq in 2014, for the first time since 2011, President Obama said, "There will be no American boots on the ground." Of course, he left out the fact that there would be Special Operations "advisers" on the ground and American air support overhead. So there we were, flying reconnaissance and Spec Ops overwatch missions in Iraq in June 2014.

And the things we saw. A woman's brain operates different from a man's. I'm all about the human experience and putting myself in other people's shoes. So as we were flying overhead, I would attempt to transport myself to what the people on the ground were experiencing. I would be three miles up in the sky, but in my mind's eye, I'd be on the ground. We would overfly the towns and villages and I'd see these markets on my sensor, and in my mind, I'd be there wandering the stalls, seeing the produce, smelling the spices, maybe even tasting the shawarma. We would spot a fair and see the crowds enjoying the carnival rides and all the rest. The majority of Iraqis were enjoying their lives. They were living a beautifully normal life. And all of a sudden, ISIS was there. They would infiltrate their neighborhoods and sporadically open fire on them. They'd take over a village, impose their regime, and if the civilians resisted the caliphate they would line people up—men, women, kids—and mow them down with firepower and bury them on the spot.

And we were forced to watch. We would be flying our missions overhead and we would detect this nefarious activity. As we hid high overhead, we would zoom in with our sensors only to get a front row seat to ISIS's atrocities. But because they were persecuting Iraqi citizens and not Americans, we were forced to sit on our hands and record the acts because the rules of engagement allowed us to defend only US citizens and coalition troops. It was heartbreaking; we couldn't do what we were trained to do—which is to protect human life. And boy were we trained. I spent nine years, one month, and ten days from the time I started at the Naval Academy training. I had a bachelor's degree, three years of flight school, and thousands of hours studying, flying the simulator, and flying training missions in my aircraft preparing for this. So here I am overhead witnessing pure evil and I can't do the thing that I was trained to do: stop it. I was trained to protect these people, and I wasn't allowed to.

That was really hard. When we were finally authorized to use lethal force, on August 8 when President Obama approved it, it was time. This wasn't about retribution. It was about doing the right thing. Protecting innocent people. Later, I would study death and killing when I returned to the Academy, and I understood intellectually the principles of dehumanizing your enemy. I knew that terrorists put bags over the heads of their captives before shooting them to remove their identity, and that shooting lines always have multiple shooters to give the perpetrators plausible deniability that it was their bullet that did the deed. But that wasn't us; we weren't there to commit crimes or act in retribution. We were there as a just military force ensuring the safety and stability of Iraq and the Iraqi people.

At the Academy, we studied the ethics of warfare. Utilitarianism justified our actions: to sacrifice the lives of a few in order to spare the lives of thousands is a good thing. Just-war theory allowed us to protect innocent life through the use of force and violence. And I was completely okay with that, because I saw the things that ISIS did. I had seen their utter disregard for human life; I had seen how brazen the terrorists were in attacking civilians.

So in my mind, *Yes, we did the right thing*.

I wish that I could say that the right thing was done to me. Coming home and dealing with the emotional side of things was tough. In the three years I spent in my squadron I never really felt like I was accepted by my squadron, or by my peers. Despite going to war with these people, I was never really given a full chance to be myself. It was kind of like being back at the Naval Academy again: conform to who we want you to be, or get out of our club.

For me—and it took a long time to realize this—that was my moral injury. I worked hard and earned my place to be there, and I should have been given a fair shot. I was raised to be accepting of others. And the frustrating thing was, I was treated different for reasons that were beyond my control. That was damning to me. Why couldn't I be accepted for who I was, to be part of the larger group?

Since sharing my story in my book and in my presentations, I've realized that I wasn't alone in feeling that way. Countless people have reached out, come up to me after my talks—veterans, some combat veterans and some not—and they've thanked me for sharing my story. They appreciate the honesty and the vulnerability, and the feeling that serving was the best thing they've ever done, but that there were parts that were a life-and-death struggle.

Still, I'd do it all over again. Because we were there to do the right thing, and I know that I did my part and returned with honor.

CHAPTER 14

SERGEANT NICK "THE REAPER" IRVING

UNITED STATES ARMY

As a sniper, you have the power to end the most precious thing on this planet without that person even being aware of your existence. It takes a certain type of individual to deal with having that kind of power.

I poked my head up to scan for targets. The noise of a round being fired snapped, and a moment later dirt and rock flew up. Seconds later the same thing happened to my spotter, Pemberton.

"It's a sniper! Sniper!" Mike yelled.

Derek, the other guy with us in that pinned down position, screamed over to us, asking us if we were hit.

We weren't but I sensed that if we didn't do something quick and smart, we were going to be taken out.

Our sniper team had been ordered to go out in support of a group of Regimental Reconnaissance Division (RECCE) Rangers. Those guys were legends and I really wanted to be a part of that elite unit. Now I was super scared that I was going to die alongside one of them. We'd split off as planned from the main element. Derek, the RECCE's squad leader, and I both had had a bad feeling as we got within a half mile of our objective. We'd decided to hunker down, sensing that we might be getting set up for an ambush. Good thing we listened to our guts, otherwise we never would have survived that initial 360-degree assault from AKs, RPK machine guns, and pistol fire.

If that wasn't bad enough, those sharp and precise cracks were coming from a sniper. A few days before, all of us had been housed for a while with a platoon of marines. Over a poker game, we were swapping stories and one marine told us to beware the Chechen. Rumor had it that he'd been around since the Soviet-Afghan days and had more than three hundred kills to his credit. Here he was, in 2009, still adding to his total. I was skeptical then, but now, pinned down in a shallow depression, I knew that the marine wasn't exaggerating about one thing—the Chechen had crazy skills as a marksman.

This was my first time being on the other end of the scope, and I didn't like the feeling one bit. His precise firing was messing with our minds; it was almost cruel.

Just before we'd gone to ground, I'd spotted three men setting up a machine gun on top of a building in the small village. We had to take them out and then take our chances with the Chechen.

★★★★★★★★★★★★★★★★★★★★★★★★★★★★★★★★★

Sergeant Nick "the Reaper" Irving earned his reputation and nickname on a remarkable tour of duty in 2009 while serving primarily as a direct action sniper in Helmand Province. While serving with the 3rd Ranger Battalion, in a period of three months he established a record by accounting for the confirmed deaths of thirty-three enemy combatants. He was the first African American sniper to serve in his battalion, and proudly followed in the footsteps of his parents, both of whom were in the army.

Nick admits to having a bad case of "SEAL-itis" as a kid, as a result of his exposure to the Charlie Sheen film *Navy Seals*. He went so far as to attend, and pass, the Navy Sea Cadet SEAL camp in Florida following his senior year in high school. It was only because during a pre-induction physical revealed his color-blindness that he was forced to give up his long-held dream. Post 9/11, the military was in need of qualified candidates, and an army recruiter sought him out after a nurse cheated for him on the color vision test, convincing him that the army's elite Ranger Regiment was essentially, as he put it, SEALs without the water.

Nick was already a well-practiced and highly skilled marksman before entering the military, but he had to overcome a serious obstacle before he could join the Ranger Battalion—his fear of heights. Completing airborne training was a major challenge, and to this day, Nick marvels at the fact that some people leap out of airplanes for enjoyment. Despite that fear, he was able to join the Rangers, and he credits his father and father's military training for straightening him out. He admits to being an angry and sometimes wayward young man who often lacked discipline and focus, except when it came to precision marksmanship and working toward his early goal of becoming a SEAL. Early on, he discovered John Plaster's influential book, *The Ultimate Sniper*. Though a few birds and a neighbor's window paid the price of his early interest in weaponry, he refined his skills and came to liken sniping to chess, with its emphasis on anticipation, prediction, and analysis. He used those high-level critical thinking skills in serving with great distinction for six years.

Since leaving the military, he has enjoyed a career as an author of two highly regarded memoirs and a series of military action novels, as a television personality, and as an instructor at HardShoot. The last one is a precision shooting company where he instructs individuals, including Olympic marksmen, in the fine art and hard science of shooting. Along with his wife, Jessica, and his son, Kaden, he resides in Texas.

★★★★★★★★★★★★★★★★★★★★★★★★★★★★★★★★★★★★

Each time Mike lifted his head, another round impacted dangerously close. I knew that if the Chechen was missing it was because he only had a partial fix on our position. Score one for us. Unfortunately, we didn't have an exact fix on his location either.

Together, the three of us formulated a plan. We were mere inches apart and decided that Derek and I would rise up simultaneously and scan a specific sector. Four eyes were better than two. We did that and a bullet hissed between our heads. We slammed our heads back into the ground and Derek let out a bloodcurdling yell. So this is what a sniper can do to people, I thought. I also realized this: I needed to think like a sniper in order to figure out where the Chechen was operating from and what the method was to the madness he was wreaking on us.

The next phase of our plan was for Mike to get better eyes on the target area I figured the Chechen was operating out of. Using the snap-bang theory—counting the time between the sounds of a weapon's discharge and its impact—I figured he was about four hundred meters away. The rest was a bit obvious. The only window open on that side of the building had to be his firing position.

Mike rolled out of the hole, I rose up and fired three quick rounds, and then Mike opened up with Win-Mag. How he did that while taking rounds that narrowly missed him was impressive. For the next several minutes rounds came at us, each one barely missing us.

We knew we had to call in air support. Unfortunately, the second platoon was also pinned down. They were within hand-to-hand or grenade range of that building. Dropping bombs on the building would have meant killing or injuring our own men. No assistance was coming. Well, it did come, in the form of a B-2 Stealth bomber dropping flares in a show of force, but the enemy wasn't falling for that.

I knew that guys were dying out there and the 360-degree fire that we'd first taken on had resumed. I was willing to have bombs dropped on us just to end the agony and take whatever casualties we had to. At that point, I could tell that the Chechen was now directing all his rounds on me. That was what I would have done. He was going down his priority list—sniper, communications guy, medic, and so on.

I wasn't alone in this dark assessment. You could hear it in the voices of the guys over the comms. We all sensed that this was it.

We were going to die. The Taliban forces were pressing in from all directions.

For a second, Mike's and my eyes met. We nodded at one another and bumped fists. This was going to be it. My throat tightened.

Then Mike's expression shifted. He told me that, screw it, we were going to get out of this mess. He said that he'd rather take his chances with the Taliban than have to face my girl, Jessica, and tell her that I'd died. He was afraid that she'd kick his ass.

LEADING BY EXAMPLE

Eight hours later, Nick, his spotter, and the rest of the men involved in that operation did get out of that mess. It took a coordinated effort to pull it off under extraordinarily difficult circumstances. Teamwork is the hallmark of any mission and Special Operations forces embody the principles that their training emphasizes.

A sniper and his spotter have a unique relationship. The two guys that I worked the most with, Mike Pemberton and Brent Alexander, and I formed a team. I knew that, having been a high school athlete and a huge sports fan my whole life, team chemistry was important. It could make you or break you. On my later deployments, I was a sniper team leader. That was my title, but that wasn't always how I looked at the situation. The thing about special operations that appealed to me, especially as a sniper team guy, was that rank didn't really matter when it came to actually being downrange and doing the missions.

For example, I was the sniper team leader, and Brent was my spotter, but we were of equal rank. He was an E5 and I was an E5. He had two more years of experience by the time he was assigned to me, but I had seen a lot more direct action sniping and a few long-range kills while he had none. When we were matched up, after Mike was injured in a fall into a deep, deep hole, we were nearing the end of our deployment. To be honest, the closer you got to that finish line, the more worried you got about getting killed, the more conservative your approach became. With Brent, he really wanted to see some action. Who could blame him? You train for years to do a job, you want to do it. So it took some getting used to him being a bit more gung-ho, more enthusiastic than Mike had been.

Not that either Mike or I had been slacking; we just were used to the job and didn't have that same kind of new guy/new experience exuberance. We'd seen a lot and done a lot. I think that more so than Mike did, I couldn't always let go of what I'd seen or done.

All of this made for some interesting adjustments and accommodations. It helped, I think, that I was always pretty informal. I always told my guys that they should call me "Irv." I never wanted them to call me "Sergeant." Even though I'd earned the nickname and the reputation as the Reaper, I wanted everyone to operate on the same level playing field. I wasn't any better than anyone. That didn't mean that I didn't carry myself with confidence, but I remained humble. One thing is for sure, if you ever say anything in the battalion that sounds like a brag, you'll never hear the end of it. Also, that was just how I was raised. Lead by example. Don't ever be your own cheerleader.

Also, I always wanted to let the guys know, whether they were my spotter or not, that I was open to feedback. I didn't know it all. I didn't always do things the best way. I made a lot of mistakes. So if I needed it, I should be corrected.

If I was wrong, I was wrong, and I should have that pointed out to me. That's what makes a great leader. With Pemberton, he was a rank lower than me, but he always felt like he could talk to me and give me his feedback. That is the only way a team can function cohesively. In my mind, Mike was just as much of a leader as I was. I liked that he would make decisions on his own and take action. That's part of our Ranger creed. Our motto is *Sua Sponte*, which is "Of their own accord." We had rules of engagement to follow, and we always did that, but as members of the sniper team, we also had a bit of autonomy. I liked having that.

THE SNIPER MENTALITY

I look back now, and I'm completely amazed at a lot of things we all did. I was scared every time we went outside the gate. Every single time. Every single firefight. That last deployment in Helmand Province I was convinced I was going to die. Maybe it was superstition, but on your last deployment after you'd made the decision to leave the military, you knew that you were either going to get shot or killed. We were experiencing way too much contact with the enemy, way too many ambushes, way too many close calls. At that point, Marjah was the Wild West. The only thing that kept me going was the guys to my left and to my right.

I think that a lot of people have this misconception about what it means to be a sniper. A lot of people are fascinated with the long-distance kill. That's kind of the romanticized version of the lone gunman out there stalking his prey. Guys do that, and that's important, but that's not the only kind of sniping that gets done. Direct-action sniping is different. You're in a firefight. Chaos is going on all around you. I saw a mix of both kinds and they required a different skill set—not entirely, but to a degree—and a different mindset. But a lot of people don't understand that as a sniper, 90 percent of your job is relaying information back to the other guys and teams and command personnel behind you. You're out in front and can see things they can't but need to. The other 10 percent of the job is being a surgeon with bullets. The way I looked at it, that first 90 percent was about helping save lives. The same with the 10 percent. You understand, because you were either informed beforehand or have determined yourself that that person has bad intent and/or has committed bad actions in the past. You sometimes know a lot about them; you sometimes don't. Regardless, you know that they are a threat. In the case of the Taliban, they were taking the lives of innocent civilians or they were taking out coalition forces.

The psychology behind being a sniper is tough to really describe. I mean, I grew up dreaming one day of being a sniper, and people could look at that and think it's a little weird. And I guess it is. Before becoming a Ranger sniper, I'd worked as a mechanic on Strykers, as an assaulter, a machine gunner, but I changed when I was a sniper. I had to learn to compartmentalize a little better. There's the technical side of that. In one of the sniper books I read as a kid, the author talked about not getting too target fixated. He stressed the idea that you don't think of the shape that you see in the scope as a full human body. Pick out a feature on that figure—a button, a hole in his clothes, something small like that—and use it as your aiming point.

I didn't think about that at the time or during all my training, but that was a way to compartmentalize mentally. You know, for every one round you fire on a human being, in training and in combat, you're either firing on a target—a nonhuman form or something else inanimate—or just firing in a direction. When I was a machine gunner, it was all about blasting rounds and rounds and rounds. So the small number of times when you actually are locking in on a human being, it is a very strange sensation.

You almost have to disconnect from being human when you sight somebody through a scope. You've made the determination that this person is someone whose life I'm going to take.

Most of the time, the people I've engaged had no idea that I was looking at them. Things on the battlefield generally happen very quickly. And maybe because as a sniper you're trained to be an observer, it's different for us sometimes. I don't think that at any other point in my experience in war did I spend five seconds, ten seconds, thirty seconds, a minute, just fixating on one thing in my field of vision. As a sniper you do that. You take things in. That gives you time to do all your calculations and that's a good thing because you aren't thinking at that point about the consequences of what you're about to do. You also have to take the time to calm down. I'll admit that, as a younger guy (I left when I was twenty-six), the thrill of doing what I was trained to do was still very strong.

So, when I was sighting on a target and getting ready to pull the trigger and then pulling it, I did experience a kind of rush. All of it was strange at first. I'd spent so much time sighting through a ten-power magnification scope at literal targets that were two-dimensional. Then, in combat, those targets had three dimensions. Nothing I trained on beforehand could prepare me for that—different angles and other things. Consciously pulling the trigger and knowing what the outcome was likely to be was definitely strange—especially at first. I'm sure that as a machine gunner or an assaulter, I'd killed people before.

This was way more intimate. In a way, I had a relationship with the people I was firing on as a sniper. I was always saying to myself early on, "This isn't real. This isn't real." That was because it both felt like it, since it was such a new experience, and it was a way to compartmentalize and focus. I'd tell myself to settle in and then squeeze the trigger. I'd hear the crack of the rifle, but then things went silent and time seemed to stop. I would watch the bullet and wonder if it was going to find its mark. I'd see a figure fall and even then I'd wonder if I'd shot him or if he was responding to a near miss and ducking for cover.

Once I saw the effect and knew that I'd killed someone, I'd get this metallic taste in my mouth, it was like a piece of my soul. I felt a weird sadness. Yeah, there was the exhilaration leading up to the moment, but not after. I may have acted like I was way into it, but the reality is that I never shot someone and felt really, really, really good about it. Some of that was the effects of the adrenaline rush reducing. I felt down, a bit of depression or sadness.

For me, it was their eyes. They never closed. I never shot someone and then saw them lying there with their eyes closed like in the movies. Their eyes always stay open. At the beginning, I told myself that was just how it was, that the last expression on their face in life was the one that was on them when they died. No face was the same, and I tried to come to terms with that moment, when the end came. And that made me think about my own life and my own possible end. What would my expression be? What was I going to look like. I tried not to think about how shocked a lot of the people I shot looked. That would make me think about what if it was going to happen to me.

I never talked to any of the other guys about these things. I never showed them, either. I just sucked it up and moved on. I would need a day or so, or just overnight and sleep it off. After that, I was ready to go again.

PUTTING THE REAPER AWAY

Anyone who sees combat is, to one extent or another, changed by the experience. For a sniper with the number of confirmed kills that

Nick had, the transition from a surgically precise taker of lives to a civilian required some deft psychological moves.

After a while, I began to think of the Reaper as a character. He wasn't me, just this guy I played in combat or in the military generally. He was the one doing all these things, he was the one who became a kind of legend, he was the one that people interacted with. I'm not making excuses, but I was young. I wanted to fit in. I enjoyed being a badass.

The truth is, when I left the military, and even at times when I was home from deployment, that badass mentality was too much for me to deal with. I felt like I had to live up to being a badass and I was scared to death that I really wasn't that way. It's hard enough living one life, but when you're living two or being two different people, things get complicated. So, I just tried to continue to be that badass, and drinking a lot helped to do that and to forget the fear of not being a badass. That's a lose-lose proposition I can see now.

Plus, the Reaper was my identity. I'd served six deployments overall. My whole identity to that point was wanting to be a soldier, a sniper, and then being those two things. And I was good at it, too. I was known for being good at it. Being that guy, that badass, that Reaper was how I was able to survive and how I was able to function in this world. I was molded by having such a life-changing experience as being in combat and serving as a sniper. And coming back home after having been all that and figuring out a way to still be all that while in the civilian arena was hard.

It was hard to fit in, definitely hard to fit in, and that's why I used alcohol to self-medicate. Was I who people thought I was? Were they seeing through my façade? Did I do what I was doing just so I could be accepted? Those questions of self-identity are really tough.

But I got it sorted out. It took having my son, Kaden, three years ago to really set me on the right path. I stopped drinking after he was born. Having a son made me put the Reaper in a box. And I stowed that box away, because that was who I was then, and this is who I want to be and am in the process of becoming now—a dad. And it was hard. He had a heart issue when he was born. My sister-in-law had just lost her infant son to a heart issue. So it was a very, very scary time. That was the most frightened I'd ever been. Combat couldn't compare. Being a dad is way more stressful than being in combat. I think seeing how fragile life is and how easily it can be taken away humbled the Reaper a little bit. Having the Reaper mentality isn't necessary with my little guy because I see the innocence in everything now. When I look through that scope, I see things very differently. I can't get time to stand still; in a blink of an eye, our child has gone from birth to three years old.

Funny thing was, not getting very good sleep, having to be hyper-vigilant all the time as a parent was harder than Ranger qualification. Now, I'm stressed by wondering if I'm being a good leader for my son. Am I doing right? I want some feedback on that, and it isn't always coming to me. I wish I had First Sergeant Seeley like I did back when I got into 3rd Ranger Battalion. He helped get me squared away back then.

He and I were the only black men in our company, Charlie Company, and he would help me deal with the awkwardness of it. He held me to a higher standard, or at least I felt like it at the time. I didn't really fully understand this at the time, but he knew what it was like to have to represent. I was the only black man and so everything I did was a reflection of me being black. I don't think I understood at the time what kind of responsibility that was and I don't think that my white platoon-mates ever had to feel that. They were just one of many, so anything they did wasn't as big a deal as something I did.

RACE AND LIFE

Recent events have given Nick a chance to reflect on what it has meant to be a black man serving in the military. Like the Reaper character he became, he felt he needed to set certain things aside once he returned to civilian life.

I've never really talked about this openly. I was too scared and too uncomfortable. Given what's happened recently with the death of George Floyd and the response to that, I've been asked about these issues more. The simple answer is that yes, in the military, I was discriminated against. It wasn't always open, so it was often subtle, but I felt it was there.

Some people made assumptions about me just because of the color of my skin. There was one guy in the platoon who would talk ghetto to me all the time. He was white and into hip-hop I guess, and he would say that he and I were "the niggas of this battalion." I would say to him, "What the heck?" He'd say, "Yeah, man, it's true." And he'd go on to talk about how he felt he was oppressed just like I was. Well, I never said I was oppressed and I never said I liked hip-hop and I never talked the way he did and he expected me to. It wasn't just him. Guys were surprised to find out that my parents were still married. They just assumed that a black family had been broken up. Nope. My parents are still together. They were both in the army. When they met my girlfriend, Jessica, who is now my wife, they were shocked to find out that she's Mexican. At least they were up front about it: "Dude, I honestly thought she was going to be a black chick with a big booty." They all assumed that, because I was black, when we went out drinking that I would, of course, drink a 40-ounce—a kind of beer that guys from the ghetto are all supposed to drink. I've never had a 40 in my life. One guy insisted on calling me, "Irv from the Streets." He didn't know a single thing about me other than my skin color. He didn't know that I grew up in the suburbs, but he automatically assumed I was from the streets.

The really weird thing was that sometimes they'd use the n-word in front of me. Maybe they thought it was a sign of respect, that they trusted me or whatever, and I didn't know how to handle the situation. They'd see the look on my face and say, "No, man, not you. You're not like that. You're different."

And that was supposed to make me feel better? Yes, I was different—from them. What was tough was that I also trusted these guys with my life and they trusted me with theirs. I would shoot and die for these guys, but, when stationed in Georgia and we all went out together to certain bars, I wouldn't get served and guys wouldn't buy me drinks in case someone else in the bar saw them doing that. "Sorry, man. You know how it is."

Truth is, I did know how it was. Truth is, in the military, I was treated better as an adult than I am as civilian. I didn't really experience much racism as a kid. I realize now, that I was pretty naïve. I remember my dad having "the talk" with me. Not the one about the birds and the bees, but the one about how I should conduct myself when I am forced to have an encounter with a law enforcement officer. I thought everybody got that talk from their fathers. I now realize they don't, just minority parents talking to minority kids about what to do so they don't end up arrested, roughed up, or dead.

When I told Jess that down the line I was going to have to have that talk with my son, she was totally confused. *What? Why? You mean . . .*

I've been pulled over by law enforcement multiple times for the same taillight that is *not* burned out. I've been paid one-third less for television appearances and other work in that industry than my white counterparts with less experience. I've been told by TV people that when I had dreadlocks, I should cut them out because my appearance was sending a negative message. Some of this stuff happened as recently as two weeks ago.

So it happens. And as a black man, you take it. Not all the time, but most of the time because you grow up aware of the consequences of not taking it. And recently, as a veteran, I've watched and listened as there's been talk of having our active duty military people being called in to help quiet unrest and arrest lawbreakers. I couldn't imagine doing that. Not to black people. Not to white people.

I enlisted to fight against foreign and domestic enemies. The average protester on the streets is not an enemy, not a terrorist. That's not the job of the 101st Airborne or the Green Berets or other military units. As a civilian, seeing that being considered or threatened is scary. I think about some of the tactics we used overseas, and I can't understand how anyone would consider using them here in this country.

And I understand the anger and the frustration. I grew up hearing stories, about young black men primarily being roughed up. We all knew it and were forced to understand that was just how it was. I wanted to see it change, but it was like an obstacle in the road that got paved over. You just drove over, got used to it, or maybe took another route around it.

I'm sad about the state of this nation right now. I really am. I remember how people rallied around the flag after 9/11. We were all on the same page. We felt unified for a while. I am proud of what I did in fighting the Global War on Terror. I'm glad I served, but in a way, with what's going on now in this country and how divided we all are, it's almost like what our Vietnam veterans faced in coming home. We aren't physically being spit on and degraded, but it is an enormous sign of disrespect for our efforts to come back home from war to have another one going on here. Especially since we can fix this.

We need to be open. If we put everything on the table, put everything out there and have real conversations, we can fix this. Just as I was nervous and frightened of opening up and talking about my negative experiences because I don't want to make anyone else feel bad or feel bad for me, we have to step up and speak up. But more than that, we need to do what I did as a sniper and as a leader. I learned to observe. I learned to listen and witness and think and then respond.

If I could tell everyone in this country one thing that I learned it would be this: We need to have an open ear and an open mind. We need to have leaders that are willing to listen, to accept feedback, and to adjust. We also need to remember that we still have men and women overseas who are fighting and dying to preserve and protect the principles that we're all supposed to have bought into as Americans.

And remember that if you have respect for a veteran, and the vast majority of people do, that means that you should have respect for yourself and for other Americans. We were all there fighting, black guys, white guys, Hispanic guys. So, if you want to say thank you for your service, then stop the fighting here, stop the discrimination among races and classes. That can start with being an open ear. Listen. As a leader, it isn't about issuing commands. You have to listen, accept feedback, and make changes.

CHAPTER 15

STAFF SERGEANT
DAVID BELLAVIA
UNITED STATES ARMY

As a Medal of Honor recipient,
my goal is to talk to parents
about why they should be giving
their sons and daughters to
provide the next generation
of soldiers to be ready for the
next great opponent we have
to take on. I want to remind
folks that America is worth it.

Death in Iraq was becoming more and more IED-related. You didn't see the enemy. They just kind of disappeared, and it was random. You got in a Humvee, you put on your iPod, and you disappeared. There was no closure when you lose friends that way.

In 2004 in Fallujah, we were involved in so many direct fire engagements. We made eye contact with the enemy. And we lost guys. That was a totally different experience, losing someone that way. You automatically had to address *Okay, not only did that just happen, but someone made this happen. That person is still here.* House fighting, especially in an urban environment, the sense you most rely on—hearing—is gone. Your eyesight, because you're so tired and hungry, diminishes. You devolve into an almost animalistic being. Like, I'm smelling this guy. I see a pristine drinking cup on a counter and everything else is covered in dust and grime. A piece of cheese sits on a plate. *There's a person here.*

You become a wolf—just sniffing the air and smelling. Everything stops. Your whole body freezes. You don't breathe. You don't think. All you do is become a single, focused thought: *There's a threat here and it needs to be put down.*

★★★

David Bellavia was the first living recipient of the Iraq War to receive our nation's highest military award, the Medal of Honor. In June 2019, at a White House ceremony, David joined America's most exclusive and heroic club. He is one of only 3,525 individuals who have earned that illustrious award since its creation in 1861. David is grateful that he was nominated and selected for his actions in the Second Battle of Fallujah in 2004, while keeping things in perspective. "I look at a guy like Bennie Adkins, who recently passed away. He was given the award in 2014 for exemplary conduct from 1965. He was serving in Laos and Cambodia at the time and those actions weren't 'authorized,' weren't a part of the declared war in Vietnam, so he had to wait a long time to be recognized. This is really a blessing." He's also quick to point out that neither the award nor his service defines who he is: "Our job was just something that we did. It was a part of our overall life experience."

A native of Buffalo, New York, David grew up the youngest of four sons. His maternal grandfather, Joseph Brunacini, had a great influence on him. Grandpa Joe served in the army during the Normandy campaign and was awarded a Bronze Star. In a family that prized education, David was a bit of an exception. His early interest in the military and combat wasn't always warmly received. "I was always told that this wasn't my role. I was too smart. We worked so hard so that you could become a dentist. *Well*, I thought, *you worked so hard so that I could have a choice.*"

Following his graduation from the University of Buffalo, David enlisted in the army in 1999. Originally assigned to a recruiting battalion so his infant son could receive medical care, David eventually became an infantryman. He served in Kosovo and Operations Iraqi Freedom I and II. David left the army in 2005 and co-founded Vets for Freedom, an advocacy group for combat veterans and their battlefield mission. He also worked as an embedded reporter in Iraq before returning to the United States, and lives in New York State with his wife and three children.

★★★★★★★★★★★★★★★★★★★★★★★★★★★★★★★★★★★★★★★

WHAT IT TAKES

What drives you to knock out that threat? When do you relax and smoke a cigarette? We were so immersed in a constant state of evaluating threat in that urban environment. And despite having to be hypervigilant, I thought that was actually easier for me than jungle or mountain warfare. There, the enemy could be hundreds or thousands of meters away and I'm going to have to use my machine gun and fire at a position until rounds stop coming from that area. Was the enemy killed? Did the enemy flee? Change position?

In that urban environment, I knew if I had been effective. I knew instantly what capabilities the enemy possessed. I could have direct impact and everyone on my squad has ownership of a death. You didn't have one guy dealing with the consequences—everyone was dealing with them. It was so much easier to compartmentalize your psychological warfare of these guys. All I had to do was tell them, "We all did this. We all put a round in this guy. We all killed him. Let's keep moving."

That was also psychologically debilitating for the enemy. Then we were back in 1943 and we were island-hopping. We were giving them the fight they didn't expect. We were supposed to be entitled Americans. We were supposed to use our lasers and our drones. And there we were, old tech, Old Testament, bashing down doors. When you see the fear in their faces, it empowers you. You feel like, *We got this. There's nothing we can't handle here.*

If the crescendo of violence is a thing, then you have to build a unit up to it. That ultimately leads to close-quarter fighting. Once you're there, you feel like Thor. There's nothing you can't do.

Then, later in life, you go to a job interview. There are twenty other candidates. You're like, *Pssh, I got this. There's nothing you can throw at me that I can't handle.* There are no RPGs being fired in here. You can't throw anything at me—disease, divorce, heartbreak, bankruptcy—you bring it, I got it. That's how we don't become victims of our experiences. We are empowered by them. Being empowered by our military service is the greatest gift you can ever receive. Knowing that you've been through worse and got through it is an amazing feeling. And you got through it because it wasn't about me. I wasn't doing it for me. I was doing it for other people. It wasn't ever about me. It was always about other people.

David's actions as a squad leader during Operation Phantom Fury in Fallujah on November 10, 2004, speak volumes about the qualities he and other members of his platoon possessed. Nearing the end of a twelve-building clearing operation, they entered a structure and came under immediate machine gun fire in a front hallway. Ambushed and effectively trapped, and with two soldiers already wounded, David's men were in dire need of assistance.

David stepped in, retrieved an automatic weapon, and first with another soldier, and then alone, according to his Medal of Honor citation, "Acting on instinct to save the members of his platoon . . . Staff Sergeant Bellavia ultimately cleared an entire enemy-filled house, destroyed four insurgents, and badly wounded a fifth. Staff Sergeant Bellavia's bravery, complete disregard for his own safety, and unselfish and courageous actions are in keeping with the finest traditions of military service and reflect great credit upon himself and the United States Army."

FACING FEARS

Nothing against SEALs and Green Berets and other Special Operations units. They're elite. But there are a lot of just average, normal guys out there that do above-average things. They're a representation of what I believe is the American ethos. It's not necessarily a warrior ethos; it's something that we have in our DNA, and we've had it from our nation's inception. We overcome fear.

People ask me, "What do you fear most in the world?" My answer is that I fear fear. I'm afraid of becoming afraid. You have to overcome it in every aspect of your life—whether that's asking that girl out on a date, applying for a job, killing a cockroach in the kitchen. There's something that you are going to have to face.

I believe that peer pressure is an incredible thing. We always seem to talk about it in negative ways. But sometimes peer pressure gets you through difficult times because it's impossible to take a step backward when everyone else is moving forward. The easiest job in the world is to lead. The most difficult job is to follow. You have to trust that guy out in front. You have to trust their guidance and do what it takes to not be the weakest link in the chain.

So, for me, that meant making myself uncomfortable every day. In my military career, as a businessman, as an adult in the civilian world, it doesn't matter—do something that you are afraid to do. I want to lift that weight to the point where my body says *Stop*. I want to read the book when my eyes are telling me *You're tired*. I want to just do something and address that fear.

You need to prepare yourself for the things you can't control that are going to come your way. The first guy to die in Fallujah was my sergeant major, Steve Faulkenburg, and this guy, we idolized him. He was from Indiana. He was our father figure. I tell civilians the teacher in the classroom is your platoon sergeant. That sergeant major is your principal. And you might not have the best relationship with him, you might only see him when you've done something wrong, but he's your mascot. He's your empathy. He's your leader. He's the guy that is emblematic of your entire unit. They are the most experienced;

they're the most grizzled. They've been everywhere, they've done everything, and they're infallible. They just are perfect in everything they do, and how could he get hit randomly? How did they pick him? What happened?

And when he dropped, we thought, *If he could die, any one of us . . .* His death was the biggest morale depleter in the universe, to lose your company commander, your company executive officer, your sergeant major, hours apart in a firefight. I sensed that some of the guys were thinking, *Man, it could happen to anyone. This is all dumb luck.*

FIGHTING WORDS

I would practice the best Knute Rockne speeches. I would write for like a day before we had a mission. And I would sit everyone down and I would just try to do the best morale building I could. And sometimes they were decent and sometimes they were just horrible, just way too much cliché, way too much.

But it was important to constantly build these guys up to realize that this is a gift. We're being given a gift. Nobody else has the opportunity. We can avenge all those people that we mourn, all those people that broke our heart when we loaded them into a bag, the thirty-seven guys up to that point that we buried. We are going to avenge every one of them, and we're going to look at their parents and we're going to be able to say, "You know what? We got that guy. I can confirm that boy who destroyed your life, who took your son away from us and you, that guy is meat. We took care of him, and we did it because of your son's sacrifice. The thing that motivated us was your son falling. Had he not given us that sacrifice, we would not have had the strength to do what we did."

The greatest lesson I learned was the ability to fire someone and to do it out of love and to do it out of concern. I was such a prick in garrison, and when we got ready to deploy, a lot of my peers were telling their squad, "Hey, you've got eleven guys. We're in Germany. The drinking age is different. There's a lot of girls there." Some of the people are married and have kids, and they're like, "Spend as much time as you can with—when we train, we're going to train hard, but spend as much time as you can with your family." And I saw it as, You have to earn that time. So I took their weekends. I took their nights. And if they snapped, if they turned, if they got obstinate, I was like, "You know what? You need to go make coffee for a battalion. You're not worthy to be here. You have to earn that freedom, because you're going to be away for over a year."

One of the things that made guys like me really unpopular is there was a mindset in the DoD with these long wars: *Let's put Burger King in our FOBs. Let's give access to videophone calls, and let's let them talk to their kids and talk to their moms and talk to their girlfriends.* And I hated that. I absolutely hated that. "I don't want you to think about Burger King. This isn't home. We're fighting to get home. I want you pissed off. I want you agitated. I want you focused. I don't want you thinking about your bills. I don't want you thinking about your girlfriend. I don't want you to think about your wife. All of those people are gone. Put them through a shredder.

"Your focus right now is the guy on the other side of the wire that wants to kill us, and I hope you've got an edge to you, and I hope you're pissed off, because I'm pissed off. And when we get the opportunity to fix one of those guys, we are going to just rage like you've never seen before. It's a video game. You're going to hit that button, and you're going to rage. It's going to be controlled, it's going to be disciplined, but it's going to be rage. And that's what I need to get through to the other side. So save your Whoppers for the pogues. Let the support guys eat their Pizza Hut. None of that—you're going to eat what I eat, you're going to suck like I'm sucking, and when we finally get the opportunity to go home, that's what you fought for, and that's when you get to let your hair down and be normal. But until that day, we are not ever going to have complacency. We're not ever going to think that *I'll just tell my mom about this*, or *I'll just check in to see what's going on with so-and-so*. Those are the guys that make mistakes." Those are the guys that don't have the will, and it was my job to focus them 100 percent.

I had a kid tell me that he feared me more than he feared the enemy. And I thought, *Man, that's the coolest thing I ever heard in my life*.

That's exactly the way it should be. Like I'm not afraid of al-Qaeda or ISIS or any of these guys. I'm afraid of my command. I'm not letting them down. I'm not going home and say, Do I have anything left? I have nothing left. I have nothing left. I have to recharge to get back out there. But when I get out there, I am going to change the course of history. The block I have to clear is going to be the Normandy Beach.

And if you're on the other side of me on that street corner, you are in for a long day. I don't know what it's like to be shot eighty-five times. I don't know what it's like to be fragged or blown up. But until that day happens, none of that is in my brain. There's no concept of dying. There's no concept of being injured. It's "you are the one." The enemy is the one that's going to suffer. And they're going to tell their kids, "Don't mess with America." Or maybe it's, "Wait, you don't know who your dad was. Oh, maybe that's because he made a poor decision and so you decide you're not going to make the same one."

LESSONS LEARNED

Hopefully, our American children will be able to get together and say, "Hey, we don't have the same culture. We don't agree. But we still really want to do what our dad did. How about we just learn to get along, because this is not something we want to repeat for another generation."

And that's fine. That's good. That's why we went there. But those future generations might be missing out. There's a beauty and an innocence to combat that you will never experience unless you are there doing it. That's watching people who have no connection whatsoever to one another coming together and being willing to do things they'd never be asked to do in the civilian world.

It's not about stopping in the rain to help change a stranger's flat tire. It's about stopping in the rain to change someone's flat tire knowing that another car is coming down the road and it's going to hit you. You still volunteer to do it.

I found that in the worst part of humanity, there's like this . . . it's just like God's grace just shows up. You actually feel the presence of God in the worst situation possible. And not just Americans, but the enemy. The enemy is doing beautiful things for each other because they're in it together. It doesn't make me want to stop shooting, but it makes me respect the hell out of them, and it changes my life forever, too. Because we're not fighting storm troopers, and we're not fighting a bunch of yahoos. We're fighting people that are into their cause, believe in their cause, and will die for their cause.

We have business on the battlefield, but when that's over, you look back and say, "I hope every person in our country can see a stranger as important as themselves." If you're willing to do things for them, I just think that's the meaning of life. I'm not going to get thanked, you're not going to know my name, you're not going to pay me, and I will still do it. The closest thing I've ever seen to God is when you see people sacrifice knowingly without any concern for themselves.

And I had to learn that didn't apply just to soldiers doing the fighting. I hated chaplains. I used to think, *Look, you want to pray? Work it out, man. I don't have the time for that. Just go. You're here to Hemingway this experience and tell all your other chaplain buddies that you were on the battlefield.* Then, the last thing my dying friends heard was a man telling them that they were loved. That is probably the most special gift you can give someone when they're dying. And had that chaplain not been there, they would have never had that peace. I wouldn't have had that peace. I can't live with knowing that my guys bled out alone on a floor in a dirty place surrounded by death. They didn't, and that Chaplain Brown, Ric Brown, he delivered souls. He risked his life to make sure our people knew that they were loved and cared for.

And I hated journalists. Same thing as with the chaplains, only worse—attention seekers. Trying to make a name for themselves. Then, an Australian reporter named Michael Ware got embedded with us. I was resistant at first, but the guy was actually with me in that building in Fallujah. I told him to get the hell out of there and stay safe, but he didn't. It was more than just him being brave. He was the observer; he was the eyes on the scene. And that was important. If it wasn't for that observer, very little of what went on would be preserved. I couldn't recommend someone for an award unless there was someone there to witness their actions and verify them. I couldn't get those kids the recognition they deserved. I was too busy changing magazines and putting dressings on blood to take note of everything.

That guy, Michael Ware, risked his life so that my friends, us regular infantry guys, us everyday Middle Americans, got some recognition. Because of him and other embedded journalists, the tradition of the 1st Infantry Division, the guys in Vietnam, the boys of Normandy, had their legacy preserved. Our tradition was ongoing.

I never really thought about legacy when I was in a fight. A legacy is what old men think about when they're dying. But now I realize how important that legacy is.

I look at those two roles in a different light. They were a part of who we are and what we did.

I was so impressed by Michael Ware that I wanted to be Michael Ware. After I retired, I went back to Iraq twice as an embedded journalist. And I saw some things I didn't like. I witnessed "balcony" journalism. Literally, I saw some broadcast journalists hanging out of balcony windows while other reporters were down in the streets in the middle of pitched battles. So, just as in anything, there were good journalists and bad journalists. Bob Woodruff was wounded by an IED. That was not supposed to happen. He's had a huge impact on my life. Like Michael Ware, Bob has a view that is 180 degrees opposed to mine. But I don't care. I stand up for both of those dudes. Michael Ware is family to me. No one will disrespect him. I've seen what he's done and what he did for me.

There are bad journalists out there, but do we focus on them or on the good ones, the ones who make the profession proud? Journalists are a huge part of why America is free. It is a huge part of who we are as a culture and a society. The good ones are carrying their weight and they're good enough to carry America.

It's important to have different perspectives, and journalism supports that. Today, everyone has an opinion about everything. COVID-19 happens, and suddenly we're all research specialists posting our findings on Facebook or wherever. What we don't do is properly consider the sources of our material, our "facts." Everyone responds emotionally to everything. We paint millennials in a bad light; the iGeneration is awful; but the truth is that my parents' generation thought the same things about us. We had PlayStation 1. We were couch potatoes; we lived in our parents' basements until we were twenty-five. Then the Twin Towers fell.

Every generation is going to be tested. And some people are going to answer the call. Fortunately, I believe that many liberals shoot as straight as conservatives. I served with a lot of guys who hated George W. Bush and his reasons for taking us to war. Now they didn't vote for President Trump. But under fire, they saved my life and they made sure I came home. Those guys are my family. I love them to death. We argue about politics every single day, but we also see beyond that.

The only way to bridge the divide is if everyone realizes that we all have skin in the game. Everyone has to serve. Does that mean they have to be in the military, that we should reinstate the draft? No. We all have to do something that's about doing something for someone other than ourselves.

And we should all realize that as soldiers, as warriors, we swore an oath of allegiance to a document, to the US Constitution. Not to a party or a president or even to our country. We were there protecting a document and what that document represents. We chose to go be uncomfortable so that others could remain in comfort. We didn't do it for our careers or our bottom line.

Cops and firemen and other first responders are part of that ethos too. We all work for the common good. And I say to everyone else, take your gifts, your talents, and do the same. If you're a cook, then cook. If you're an organizer, organize. But let's all pull on the same rope. We were born on the same side. Let's stay there. Let's keep doing what our generation, my generation did. Let's all find that thing like we did in our military service. Let's find our true north.

APPENDIX OF MODERN WARRIORS
— ★ ★ ★ —

★ STAFF SERGEANT DAVID BELLAVIA, UNITED STATES ARMY ★

* **Awards and Honors**
  * Medal of Honor
  * Bronze Star
  * Army Commendation Medal (2)
  * Army Achievement Medal (2)
  * New York State Conspicuous Service Cross
  * New York Veterans' Hall of Fame inductee
* **Units served with:** 2nd Battalion, 2nd Infantry Regiment, 1st Infantry Division
* **Years of service:** 1999–2005
* **Combat deployments:** Iraq War
* Co-founded Vets for Freedom, a political advocacy group.
* Authored the memoir *House to House: An Epic Memoir of War* in 2007.
* After retiring from the military, briefly served as an embedded reporter in Iraq.
* David is a longtime Buffalo Bills fan.

★ SERGEANT MAT BEST, UNITED STATES ARMY ★

* Awards and Honors
  * Ranger Tab
  * Army Commendation Medal with Valor (3)
  * Army Achievement Medal (2)
  * Combat Infantryman Badge
  * Parachutist Badge
* **Units served with:** 2nd Ranger Battalion, 75th Ranger Regiment
* **Years of service:** 2004–2008
* **Combat deployments:** Iraq War (5), War in Afghanistan
* Served for five years as a private contractor in hostile areas around the world.
* Earned a bachelor's degree in liberal arts with magna cum laude honors.
* Post-military, Mat and fellow veteran Jarred Taylor co-founded Article 15 clothing brand.
* Mat also serves as executive vice president of Black Rifle Coffee, an enterprise he co-founded with former Green Beret Evan Hafer.
* Matt has more than three million subscribers across social media platforms, with all his channels hitting nearly a billion views combined.
* Mat's father and two brothers all served in the US Marine Corps.
* Mat's groundbreaking memoir, *Thank You for My Service*, became a *New York Times* bestseller in 2019.

★ LIEUTENANT COMMANDER (RET.) DANIEL CRENSHAW, UNITED STATES NAVY ★

* Awards and Honors
  * Bronze Star with Valor
  * Bronze Star
  * Joint Commendation Medal
  * Army Achievement Medal
  * Combat Action Ribbon (2)
  * Purple Heart
  * Navy and Marine Corps Commendation Medal with Valor
* **Units served with:** United States Navy SEALs, SEAL Team 3, Special Reconnaissance Team 1
* **Years of service:** 2006–2016
* **Combat deployments:** Iraq War (2), War in Afghanistan
* While serving in Helmand Province, he lost his right eye in an IED explosion.
* He returned to complete tours of duty in South Korea and Bahrain following his recuperation from those severe injuries.
* He was medically retired in 2016.
* In 2017 he earned his master's degree in public administration from Harvard University's Kennedy School of Government.
* He is a proud sixth-generation Texan and currently is a member of the US House of Representatives serving the people of Texas's Second District.
* He recently released the book *Fortitude: American Resilience in the Era of Outrage*, which became a *New York Times* bestseller.

★ CAPTAIN (RET.) CHAD FLEMING, UNITED STATES ARMY ★

* Awards and Honors
  * Bronze Star with Valor with Oak Leaf Cluster (2 Bronze Stars)
  * Purple Heart with 2 Oak Leaf Clusters (3 Purple Hearts)
  * Meritorious Service Medal
  * Army Commendation Medal with Valor 5 Oak Leaf Clusters (6 ARCOMS)
  * Army Ranger Tab
  * Combat Infantryman's Badge
  * Senior Parachutist Badge
  * Air Assault Badge
  * Expert Infantryman's Badge
* **Units served with:** 4th Infantry Division, 3/75th Ranger Regiment, 3/75th Ranger Reconnaissance Platoon, 75th Ranger Regiment HHC
* **Years of service:** 1998–2011
* **Combat deployments:** Iraq War (6), War in Afghanistan (5)
* He was wounded three times and endured more than 20 surgical procedures including the trans-tibial amputation of his left leg.
* Captain Fleming redeployed 5 times after his injuries, each time going right back into the fight. He is one of the few amputees who have been able to redeploy into combat as an amputee.
* After receiving therapy and rehabilitation at the Center for the Intrepid in San Antonio, Texas, he has competed in 5K runs, triathlons and a 360-mile bike ride from San Antonio to Dallas, Texas, all as an amputee. He rode his Trek bicycle from San Francisco to Los Angeles (480 miles) in October 2008 and completed the New York City Marathon in 2009.
* After Captain Fleming retired from active duty he continued to serve our country in other capacities.

★ SERGEANT MAJOR (RET.) ERIC JOSEPH GERESSY, UNITED STATES ARMY ★

* Awards and Honors
  * Silver Star
  * Bronze Star with 2 Oak Leaf Clusters (3 Bronze Stars)
  * Meritorious Service Medal with 2 Oak Leaf Clusters
  * Army Commendation Medal with Valor with 4 Oak Leaf Clusters
  * Defense Superior Service Medal
  * Iraqi Campaign Medal (5)
  * Valorous Unit Award
  * Combat Infantryman Badge
* **Units served with:** Bravo Company, 2nd Battalion, 187th Infantry, 101st Airborne Division (Air Assault); Charlie Company, 3rd Battalion, 187th Infantry, 101st Airborne Division (Air Assault); Eagle Company, 2nd Squadron, 2nd Stryker Calvary Regiment; HHC Recon Platoon, 1–506th Infantry (Air Assault), 2nd Infantry Division; Charlie Company, 1–504th Parachute Infantry Regiment, 82nd Airborne Division; Charlie Company, 2nd Battalion, 27th Infantry, 25th Infantry Division (Light); HHC Recon Platoon, 1st Battalion, 509th Parachute Infantry Regiment; United States Southern Command
* **Years of service:** 1988–2014
* **Combat deployments:** Iraq War (3)
* 26 years of active federal service in the US Army with more than 11 years of overseas service.
* After his retirement from the army, Eric earned a master's degree in intelligence studies from American Military University.
* A proud New Yorker from Staten Island, Eric's father worked for the New York Police Department.

* Several members of his family served in the US Army with distinction, including a great-uncle, Rosario Squatrito, who also earned a Silver Star as a member of the OSS.

* Eric's story is featured in the book *American Warfighter: Brotherhood, Survival, and Uncommon Valor in Iraq, 2003–2011* by J. Pepper Bryars.

* Eric now works as a contractor for the Department of Defense.

★ SERGEANT NICK "THE REAPER" IRVING, UNITED STATES ARMY ★

* Awards and Honors
  * Ranger Tab
  * Army Commendation Medal
  * Afghanistan Campaign
  * Joint Service Achievement Medal (JSAM)
  * Joint Commendation Medal
  * Army Achievement Medal
  * Army Commendation Medal with Valor
* **Units served with:** 75th Army Ranger Regiment, 3rd Ranger Battalion
* **Years of service:** 2004–2010
* **Combat deployments:** Iraq War, War in Afghanistan
* Recognized for having 33 enemies killed in action in a 3.5-month span in Afghanistan.
* He was the first African American to serve as a sniper in 3rd Ranger Battalion to deploy to the Global War on Terrorism.
* Nick now works on various TV and movie productions, as well as writing and publishing under his own company.
* He is the author of the *New York Times* bestselling memoir *The Reaper* and its follow-up, *Way of the Reaper*.
* He is also the author of a successful series of military novels: *Reaper: Threat Zero*, *Reaper: Ghost Target*, and *Reaper: Drone Strike*.
* Nick served as a coach on the reality TV show *American Grit* with John Cena and as host of *Master of Arms* on Discovery.
* Nick is a recurring guest on the YouTube channel *Demolition Ranch*.
* He worked as an on-set adviser for the 2017 sniper movie *The Wall*.
* Born in Maryland, he now resides in Texas and continues to be a Dallas Cowboy fan.

★ LIEUTENANT COMMANDER CAROLINE JOHNSON, ★
UNITED STATES NAVY

* Awards and Honors
    * Navy Marine Corps Commendation Medal
    * Navy Marine Corps Achievement Medal
    * Air Medal with Strike Flight Award (2)
    * Navy Meritorious Unit Commendation
    * Afghanistan Campaign Medal
    * Global War on Terrorism Expeditionary
    * Navy "E" Ribbon
    * Sea Service Deployment Ribbon
    * Global War on Terrorism Service Medal

* **Units served with:** VFA-213 The World-Famous Fighting Black-lions, United States Naval Academy Leadership Ethics and Law Division

* **Years of service:** USNA 2005–2009, 2009–2019 Active Duty; 2019–Present Selective Reserve

* **Combat deployments:** Iraq War, War in Afghanistan

* Caroline is a 2009 graduate of the US Naval Academy.

* Caroline was a Weapon Systems Officer flying in the F/A-18F Super Hornet.

* She finished at the top of her class at flight school and was awarded the Paul F. Lawrence award as the number one strike fighter graduate.

* At the Blacklions, Caroline completed her Strike Fighter Weapons and Tactics level II, III, and IV qualifications, she earned her Combat Mission Commander designation, and she also graduated with honors from the University of Oklahoma with a Master of Arts in Administrative Leadership.

* Executed 42 combat missions in direct action against ISIS and Taliban forces in Iraq, Syria, and Afghanistan, and accrued more than 990 flight hours in the F/A-18F.

* She returned to the US Naval Academy to serve as a Senior Leadership Instructor and Aviation Operations Officer.

* She is the author of *Jet Girl: My Life in War, Peace, and the Cockpit of the Navy's Most Lethal Aircraft*.

* Today, Caroline, aka "Jet Girl," is a much-in-demand public speaker and lecturer at University of Chicago Harris School of Public Policy.

★ STAFF SERGEANT (RET.) JOHNNY "JOEY" JONES, ★
UNITED STATES MARINE CORPS

* Awards and Honors
  * Purple Heart
  * Navy Commendation Medal with Valor
  * Combat Action Ribbon
  * Presidential Unit Citation
  * First annual Active Duty Congressional Fellow for House Veterans Affairs Committee
  * Georgetown University Class of '14 Utraque Unum Spirit of Service
* **Units served with:** 1st Marine Division, 1st Explosive Ordnance Disposal Company; 3rd Marines, 1st Battalion; 2nd Marines, 2nd Battalion
* **Years of service:** 2005–2012
* **Combat deployments:** Iraq War, War in Afghanistan
* He was the first member of his family to graduate from high school.
* He graduated first of his class from the Marine Corps Communication-Electronics School.
* He served as a member of an Explosive Ordnance Disposal unit.
* Wounded by an IED in Afghanistan in 2010, he lost both legs.
* He appeared in the Academy Award–Winning film *Lincoln*.
* Through NASCAR and various charities he's gotten behind-the-scenes glimpses of stock car racing.
* Joey is a die-hard follower of his home-state Georgia Bulldogs.
* Joey currently works as a contributor for the Fox News Channel.
* He served as CEO of the Boots Campaign.
* He married his high school sweetheart.

★ LIEUTENANT COLONEL ADAM KINZINGER, UNITED STATES AIR FORCE ★

* Awards and honors
  * United States Air Force Airman's Medal (6)
  * Meritorious Service Medal
  * Humanitarian Service Medal
  * Meritorious Unit Award
  * Air Force Outstanding Unit Award (6)
  * National Guard's Valley Forge Cross for Heroism
  * Southeastern Wisconsin American Red Cross Hero of the Year
* **Units served with:** Air Force Special Operations Command, Air Combat Command; Air Mobility Command, Air National Guard, 128th Air Refueling Wing, 115th Fighter Wing; 45th Expeditionary Special Operations Squadron
* **Years of service:** 2003–present
* **Combat deployments:** Iraq War, War in Afghanistan
* In 1998, while a student at Illinois State University, he ran a successful campaign for a seat on the McLean County board.
* He resigned from that position to join the United States Air Force.
* He was twice deployed to and flew missions in Iraq.
* He continues to serve in the Air National Guard.
* Adam is currently serving his fifth term in the United States House of Representatives from Illinois's Sixteenth District.
* He is a member of both the Energy and Commerce and Foreign Affairs Committees.
* He is an avid fan of historic military aircraft, aka warbirds.

★ LIEUTENANT (RET.) MORGAN LUTTRELL, UNITED STATES NAVY ★

* Awards and Honors
  * Combat Action Ribbon (2)
  * Navy Expert Rifle Medal
  * Navy Expert Pistol Medal
  * Sea Service Deployment Ribbons
  * Good Conduct Medals (2)
  * Operation Iraqi Freedom/Operation Enduring Freedom Medal
* **Units served with:** SEAL Delivery Team 1, ST-5, ST-8, ST-10 NSWG-4
* **Years of service:** 2000–2014
* **Combat deployments:** Iraq War, War in Afghanistan
* He earned an undergraduate degree from Sam Houston State University in psychology and philosophy.
* Experienced multiple combat deployments.
* In 2009 he suffered severe injuries in a helicopter crash during a training operation off the coast of Virginia Beach, Virginia.
* Injuries: Multiple spinal fractures, Traumatic Brain Injury.
* Because of that experience, upon retirement after 14 years of service, he pursued an advanced degree in applied cognition and neuroscience from the University of Texas at Dallas and graduated with honors.
* After graduation he worked as a research scientist at the Center for Brain Health at the University of Texas at Dallas.
* In 2017 Morgan received his appointment to the Department of Energy as senior adviser to the secretary.
* He recently completed his executive education at Harvard Business School focused on professional leadership development.

★ LIEUTENANT COLONEL (RET.) SCOTT MANN, UNITED STATES ARMY ★

* Awards and Honors
  * Bronze Star
  * Meritorious Service Medal
  * Combat Infantryman's Badge
* **Units served with:** 7th Special Forces Group
* **Years of service:** 1991–2013
* **Combat deployments:** Iraq War, War in Afghanistan
* He is a 1990 graduate of the University of Central Arkansas.
* He earned his master's degree in 2005 from the Air Command and Staff College.
* From 1996 to 2006, he served with the 7th Special Forces group in Ecuador, Colombia, Peru, Panama, and Afghanistan.
* In 2015 he founded The Heroes Journey, a nonprofit organization dedicated to helping veterans share their stories as an act of healing and to connect veterans and civilians at a community level to better America.
* In 2015 he founded Rooftop Leadership as a way to help others learn how to establish trust and build relationships in high-stakes, competitive environments.
* He is the author of the book *Game Changers: Going Local to Defeat Violent Extremists*.
* He wrote and performed in the play *Last Out: Elegy of a Green Beret*. The play features veterans and members of veterans' families in the cast, and has had production runs in Florida and New York City.

★ CAPTAIN (RET.) SEAN PARNELL, UNITED STATES ARMY ★

* Awards and Honors
  * Bronze Star with Valor
  * Purple Heart
  * Combat Infantryman Badge
* **Units served with:** 3rd Platoon, Bravo Company, 2nd Battalion, 87th Infantry Regiment, 3rd Brigade Combat Team, 10th Mountain Division
* **Years of service:** 2004–2010
* **Combat deployments:** War in Afghanistan
* Was medically retired from the military due to his injuries.
* Post-military, he co-founded the American Warrior Initiative.
* He authored the *New York Times* bestseller *Outlaw Platoon: Heroes, Renegades, Infidels, and the Brotherhood of War in Afghanistan*.
* He is also the co-author of the Eric Steele series of novels: *Man of War*, *All Out War*, and *One True Patriot*.
* He worked to pass the Mission Act, which President Trump signed into law in 2018, and which helps give veterans greater access to health care in VA facilities and the community, expands benefits for caregivers, and improves the VA's ability to retain and hire the best medical professionals.
* In the November 2020 elections, he is running to represent Pennsylvania's 17th District in our nation's House of Representatives.

★ SERGEANT FIRST CLASS (RET.) JOHN WAYNE WALDING, ★ UNITED STATES ARMY

* Awards and Honors
  * Silver Star
  * Bronze Star
  * Purple Heart
  * Army Commendation Medal (3)
  * Army Achievement Medal (2)
  * Combat Infantryman Badge
  * Airborne/Air Assault
  * Special Forces Tab
* **Units served with:** 3rd Special Forces Group; ODA 3336; 3rd Special Forces Group Sniper Detachment
* **Years of service:** 2001–2013
* **Combat deployments:** Iraq War, War in Afghanistan
* On April 6, 2008, he lost his leg to an enemy sniper during the Battle of Shok Valley. That harrowing battle was recounted in the book *No Way Out: A Story of Valor in the Mountains of Afghanistan* by Mitch Weiss and Kevin Maurer.
* Post-injury, he attended the Special Forces Sniper Course and upon graduation became the first amputee ever to become a Green Beret sniper.
* He lives his life by the motto "Lean forward, fight hard."
* Today he is the CEO/founder of Gallantry Global Logistics, a service-disabled veteran-owned logistics company whose mission is to hire veterans. He is also co-founder of Live to Give, a bottled water company that gives 50 percent of its net profits to veteran and first-responder charities.

* John continues to compete in endurance events. He has:
  * finished 4th overall in the Boston Marathon in the hand-crank division.
  * finished in the top 10 in the New York City Marathon.
  * run the Army Ten-Miler.
  * completed 2017 and 2018 Bataan Memorial Death March with 45-pound rucksack. This was dubbed one of the hardest marathon routes in North America.
  * ran the 2017 and 2019 Dallas Half Marathons and 2018 marathon.

★ LIEUTENANT COMMANDER (RET.) JOHN "JOCKO" WILLINK, ★ UNITED STATES NAVY

* Awards and Honors
  * Silver Star
  * Bronze Star with Combat Distinguishing Device
  * Meritorious Service Medal
  * Navy and Marine Corps Commendation Medal
  * Combat Action Ribbon
  * Navy Unit Commendation Ribbon
  * Navy and Marine Corps Achievement Medal
  * Navy Meritorious Unit Commendation Ribbon
* **Units served with:** United States Navy SEALs, SEAL Team 3, SEAL Team 2, SEAL Team 7; Commanded SEAL Team 3's Task Unit Bruiser
* **Years of service:** 1990–2010
* **Combat deployments:** Iraq War
* Graduate of BUD/S class 177.
* Graduate of Officer Candidate School in 1998.
* Post-retirement, he co-founded Echelon Front, a leadership consultancy firm.
* He co-authored, with former SEAL team member Leif Babin, the bestselling book *Extreme Ownership: How U.S. Navy SEALs Lead and Win*.
* His other books are:
  * *Discipline Equals Freedom: Field Manual*
  * *The Dichotomy of Leadership: Balancing the Challenges of Extreme Ownership to Lead and Win*
  * *Leadership Strategy and Tactics: Field Manual*

* *The Code. The Evaluation. The Protocols: Striving to Become and Eminently Qualified Human*

* *Mikey and the Dragons* (for children)

* Way of the Warrior Kid children's series

* He is also the host of *The Jocko Podcast.*

★ STAFF SERGEANT (RET.) JEREMIAH WORKMAN, ★ UNITED STATES MARINE CORPS

* Awards and Honors
  * Navy Cross
  * Member of the Ohio Military Hall of Fame
* **Units served with:** Weapons Company, 3rd Battalion, 5th Marine Regiment
* **Years of service:** 2001–2010
* **Combat deployments:** Iraq War
* He is a strong advocate for honesty about and treatment of post-traumatic stress disorder.
* Previously served in the Marine Corps' Wounded Warrior program serving injured veterans.
* He is the author of *Shadow of the Sword: A Marine's Journey of War, Heroism, and Redemption.*
* Today he works as a military services coordinator for the Veterans Administration at a Naval Health Clinic.

RESOURCES AND ORGANIZATIONS FOR VETERANS

— ★ ★ ★ —

The Pipe Hitter Foundation
https://pipehitterfoundation.org

Mission: Our mission is simple: Serve those who serve us. The Pipe Hitter Foundation is committed to defending the rights and freedoms of our men and women in uniform—the same rights and freedoms they risk their lives to uphold. To fulfill this mission, The Pipe Hitter Foundation has the following broad goals:

- Financial support and legal defense
- Advocacy
- Public affairs

The Heroes Journey: Warriors Finding Their Voice and Telling Their Story in Transition
https://www.theheroesjourney.org

Mission: Every year, hundreds of thousands of veterans and first responders transition from service into civilian life. It's a challenging time that often results in loss of identity and changes so significant it seems like they are changing planets. For our warriors to live the life of prosperity they deserve, they must rediscover their voice and tell their story.

Boot Campaign
https://bootcampaign.org

Mission: At Boot Campaign, our mission is to unite Americans to honor and restore the lives of veterans and military families through individualized, life-improving programs.

Among its many programs, Boot Campaign assists veterans to help them reclaim health and wellness, restore families, restart careers, reduce suicide, and reinforce communities.

Sentinels of Freedom
https://www.sentinelsoffreedom.org

Mission: Our mission is to provide severely wounded post-9/11 veterans with comprehensive personal support and financial assistance as they complete their higher education and achieve success in their post-military careers.

Green Beret Foundation
https://greenberetfoundation.org

Mission: At the Green Beret Foundation, we honor our commitment to Green Berets past and present by providing Special Forces soldiers and their families with emergency, immediate, and ongoing support.

Warrior's Weekend
https://www.warriorsweekend.org

Mission: Founded in 2007, Warrior's Weekend is a non-profit, 501 (c) 3 Corporation dedicated to the support of veterans of the United States of America with an emphasis on those wounded in the Global War on Terrorism. This is accomplished through holding an annual fishing event for wounded military personnel in May in Port O'Connor, Texas, as well as donations to veterans and veterans-based causes.

Team Never Quit
https://teamneverquit.com

Mission: Team Never Quit embodies the heart of a warrior, men and women in all walks of life who have faced incredible hardship but have chosen not only to survive, but to learn from the experience and make themselves and those around them stronger for it. Our commitment is to honor those who have fallen, stand with those who have survived, and share their stories that we might inspire others to never quit.

Our brand supports these three pillars:

1. Learning from hardship

2. Becoming stronger ourselves

3. Making others stronger

Camp Southern Ground
https://www.campsouthernground.org

Mission: At Camp Southern Ground, we are dedicated to serving veterans struggling with transition from active service to civilian life, and those struggling with post-traumatic stress.

Our veteran programs, Warrior Week and Warrior PATHH, are founded on the premise that when men and women enlist to protect our country, we have an obligation to honor their service and sacrifice, and care for them upon their return home.

Stay In Step Brain and Spinal Cord Injury Recovery Center
https://www.stayinstep.org

Mission: We are a veteran-founded and -run organization that provides long-term rehabilitation and therapy to both veterans and civilians that suffer from a spinal cord and/or traumatic brain injury, or any other neurological disorder resulting in paralysis.

Travis Manion Foundation
https://www.travismanion.org

Mission: TMF empowers veterans and families of fallen heroes to develop character in future generations. Our vision is to create a nation of purpose-driven individuals and thriving communities that is built on character.

ACKNOWLEDGMENTS

— ★ ★ ★ —

Without the warriors in these pages, this book and our freedoms are not possible. This book is theirs, not mine. Thank you to each of them, their brothers-in-arms, their families, and every American who loves and supports them. I certainly remember all those I served with. With every page, we also remember those who did not make it home—purchasing our freedom at the cost of their earthly lives. God bless our fallen warriors. We remember them all, always.

Thank you to the FOX News Channel, and FOX Nation specifically, for affording me the platform to share the stories of our *Modern Warriors*. The show has been well produced, and powerfully received—because the warriors, and their experiences, are the story. Thank you to the producers who have worked on those specials, and everyone at FOX Nation who helped turn them into this book. Thank you to Suzanne Scott, Jay Wallace, John Finley, Jason Klarman, Michael Tammero, Jennings Grant, Jennifer Hegseth, and many more. Without all of you, there is no show, and no book. *Thank you*.

Thank you to Gary Brozek, who did the bulk of the legwork for this project. Gary turned all of these interviews into compelling chapters, bringing to life these amazing warriors. Thank you for your love of country, your passion for veterans, and your attention to detail. This was a huge project, and you tackled it to the ground with rigor, hard work, and professionalism.

Finally, I'm grateful to all our friends at HarperCollins who helped make this book possible. I am honored to be part of the inaugural project for this partnership with FOX News Books. Thank you for investing in this book, these warriors, and our great republic.